More Praise for *Predictive Evaluation*

"Dave Basarab's *Predictive Evaluation* approach is unique in its emphasis on predicting, and then measuring, leading indicators—intention and adoption—rather than just waiting for final results. This innovative approach shortens the continuous improvement cycle, allows learning organizations to respond more quickly to opportunities and issues, and produces greater value more quickly."
—**Roy Pollock, Chief Learning Officer, Fort Hill Company**

"Dave Basarab has succeeded in identifying a realistic way to evaluate training. Having the three elements—intention evaluation, adoption evaluation, and impact evaluation—gives the training community the ability to measure training's effectiveness throughout the process. The challenges we all have had to face when attempting an ROI model are addressed in Dave's book. I found *Predictive Evaluation* engaging, practical, and insightful."
—**Charleen Allen, Director, Global Learning & Development, Baker Hughes, Inc.**

"*Predictive Evaluation* is an innovative and at the same time practical, step-by-step guide to training evaluation. Full of Dave Basarab's keen insights into the link between training success and evaluation, it clearly illustrates how to integrate training 'intention, adoption, and impact' to get the results you want. Its wisdom, applicable to both new and existing training programs, is especially relevant in these challenging economic times. Basarab's evaluation processes are by far the best way to ensure the business value of all of your training initiatives."
—**Diana Whitney, President, Corporation for Positive Change, and coauthor of** *Appreciative Leadership* **and** *The Power of Appreciative Inquiry*

"It is becoming increasingly more critical to demonstrate value when investing resources in training programs. Dave's method offers a tangible way to assess a program's impact to the bottom line before spending the money, which gives significant credibility to training professionals."
—**Lily Prost, Global Director of People and Organization Development, Merial Limited**

"*Predictive Evaluation* provides step-by-step guidance to the novice as well as the experienced practitioner in how to make data-driven decisions about the value and worth of a program. Dave Basarab is providing a real service to those who struggle to show their training is making a difference."
—**Marguerite J. Foxon, Principal, Performance Improvement Consulting**

"*Predictive Evaluation* is more than just a training measurement guide; it is a valuable ROI tool for executive educators and business leaders alike. That's why it's a must-read."
—**John Sullivan, Project Director, Duke Corporate Education**

"Dave provides clear and easy-to-follow step-by-step instructions on how to make sure that all your good needs analysis and effective instructional design are put to use in service of having the desired impact on your organization. He describes specific processes to be sure that the right data is uncovered, the details are specified, and external factors impacting value are recognized and considered. He provides detailed guidelines on how to collect and analyze data related to adoption of new skills, knowledge, and behavior. This book will help anyone struggling to show the value of training—before the training has been implemented and after."

—**Christy Pines, Manager, Learning Services, Canon USA**

"Dave Basarab has created a unique approach to measure training ROI and found a powerful way to calculate how training investments can be linked to business results. This book is a must-read for any learning leader who wants to have a seat at the executive table."

—**Bjorn Billhardt, CEO, Enspire Learning, Inc.**

"We all know the adage 'Start with the end in mind.' This book helps us apply that concept when evaluating training and in so doing enables us to continuously target improvements in training programs as well as measure the impact of training to the bottom line of our business. A unique and useful approach to training evaluation."

—**Dr. Debby King-Rowley, Director, Burlington Group, Melbourne, Australia**

"In 1999 David van Adelsberg and Edward A. Trolley wrote a book titled *Running Training Like a Business*. Now my former colleague Dave Basarab has added new insights and tools in this book. It is a must-read for all executives looking to make solid, mindful decisions about the development of their people and the impact training will have on their business results."

—**John Marohl, Senior Consultant, Marohl Consulting, Inc.**

Predictive Evaluation

Predictive Evaluation

Ensuring Training Delivers Business and Organizational Results

Dave Basarab

Berrett–Koehler Publishers, Inc.
San Francisco
a BK Business book

Berrett-Koehler Publishers, Inc.

235 Montgomery Street, Suite 650

San Francisco, CA 94104-2916

Tel: (415) 288-0260 Fax: (415) 362-2512   www.bkconnection.com

Ordering Information

Quantity sales. Special discounts are available on quantity purchases by corporations, associations, and others. For details, contact the "Special Sales Department" at the Berrett-Koehler address above.

Individual sales. Berrett-Koehler publications are available through most bookstores. They can also be ordered directly from Berrett-Koehler: Tel: (800) 929-2929; Fax: (802) 864-7626; www.bkconnection.com

Orders for college textbook/course adoption use. Please contact Berrett-Koehler: Tel: (800) 929-2929; Fax: (802) 864-7626.

Orders by U.S. trade bookstores and wholesalers. Please contact Ingram Publisher Services, Tel: (800) 509-4887; Fax: (800) 838-1149; E-mail: customer.service@ingrampublisherservices.com; or visit www.ingrampublisherservices.com/Ordering for details about electronic ordering.

Berrett-Koehler and the BK logo are registered trademarks of Berrett-Koehler Publishers, Inc.

Printed in the United States of America

Berrett-Koehler books are printed on long-lasting acid-free paper. When it is available, we choose paper that has been manufactured by environmentally responsible processes. These may include using trees grown in sustainable forests, incorporating recycled paper, minimizing chlorine in bleaching, or recycling the energy produced at the paper mill.

Library of Congress Cataloging-in-Publication Data

Basarab, David J.

  Predictive evaluation : ensuring training delivers business and organizational results / Dave Basarab. — 1st ed.

    p. cm.

  Includes bibliographical references and index.

  ISBN 978-1-60509-824-1 (alk. paper)

  1. Employees—Training of—Evaluation. I. Title.

  HF5549.5.T7B2937 2011

  658.3'124—dc22   2010042557

First Edition

15 14 13 12 11   10 9 8 7 6 5 4 3 2 1

Cover design: Leslie Waltzer, Crowfoot Design

This book is dedicated to
My family, and especially my wife, Ann,
for all they have taught me
Dr. Marguerite Foxon, for being such
a good friend and inspiration
My colleagues, for their support
and guidance over the years
J. Bruce Hunsicker, for all the good
you have done—you left us too soon

Contents

Foreword

When I (Don) wrote my first book on training evaluation (*Evaluating Training Programs: The Four Levels*, San Francisco: Berrett Koehler, 1993), Dave contributed the introduction and a case study on how Motorola had been applying the Kirkpatrick Four Levels on a global basis. Since then, Dave has continued to dedicate himself to helping the training and development field strive to make significant contributions to its business counterparts. It comes as no surprise that this book continues in that tradition.

Predictive Evaluation takes a different look at the topic of training evaluation by adding the element of prediction. If you are accurate in your needs assessments, and if you select the correct participant behaviors to leverage desired results, Dave provides examples, templates, and formulas to actually look into the future to determine how best to make training and evaluation investments. When you use his four-step process, the lessons you learn will be invaluable for addressing business needs in a cost-effective manner, including training as one of many business-driving interventions.

A very positive aspect of Dave's approach is that it mirrors our own by focusing on powerful factors in addition to training. Rather than just mentioning these factors, Dave offers a framework to be used to determine to what degree training actually helps meet business needs. He also details how performance and impact can be maximized through the use of enablers, continuous improvement methods, lessons learned, and dashboards—after training has been completed.

A final and refreshing aspect of *Predictive Evaluation* is that Dave has included many ideas for involving the training participants, rather than just leaving the application, reinforcement, and evaluation work to training and business leaders. He has captured the truth that the more participants are involved in their own learning and performance, the more they bring about success for themselves and their organizations.

As the book states, "this approach allows training and development professionals, along with key decision makers, to predict results before program delivery and to judge the attractiveness of training using a cost/benefit approach."

We at Kirkpatrick Partners are always pleased to see ambassadors of the Kirkpatrick Model move in new and diverse directions. We are all striving for the same ultimate outcome—for training groups to bring significant, recognized value to organizations.

Donald L. Kirkpatrick, PhD, and
James D. Kirkpatrick, PhD
Kirkpatrick Partners

Preface

Do you struggle with defining the success of training?

Are you constantly fighting the battle to show and justify the value that training is bringing to your organization?

Does your organization view training as an expense versus an investment with predicted return?

Do you need to link training with the value it produces for your company?

Do you need a method of predicting (forecasting) the value of training to help decide whether to train?

Are your current evaluation efforts always after the fact—do you need a way to measure success using leading indicators that drive continuous improvement?

If you answer yes to any of these questions, this book is for you. It is written by an experienced evaluator/training professional who has dealt with and solved the challenges just mentioned. This book provides a new perspective for evaluators/training professionals looking to break new ground, to try new things, or even to breathe life into floundering projects. Some advice is very specific—some much more general. But all of it is useful to someone who wishes to improve training evaluations.

This book is filled with a series of worked examples, tips, tools, and techniques designed to enhance your training evaluations—specifically, using the Predictive Evaluation (PE) approach. This book covers a lot of territory, from data collection and analysis to reporting and continuous improvement efforts. It lays out the process of PE step by step, allowing even novice practitioners to implement much, if not all, of its contents. This book is practical—a "how-to" publication that begins where most evaluation books end. In addition to the core PE concepts, you learn the steps and tasks required for performing all elements of a PE: Predicting Value, Intention Evaluation, Adoption Evaluation, and Impact Evaluation. Furthermore, all required PE tools, whether forms or worksheets (with completed examples), are provided. Finally, to reinforce each step's concept and task, a worked example is provided to show the desired output. This is a handbook for practitioners: its primary purpose is to provide the steps and tools required to undertake PE.

This approach allows training and development professionals, along with key decision makers, to predict results before program delivery and to judge the attractiveness of training using a cost/benefit approach. Based on predicted impact, key decision makers can make informed decisions on their training investment and decide whether to proceed. If they decide to move forward, PE evaluates Intention, Adoption, and Impact against the forecast and implements corrective actions as needed when results fall below success gates. PE moves the measurement of training and development from a set of activity-based measures to value-driven continuous improvement efforts that ensure that training investments create their predicted value.

The value of this book is in its handbook approach: it is a collection of instructions, steps, examples, and procedures providing a ready reference for performing PE. This book is designed to be easily consulted for quick answers about PE. You don't need a degree in evaluation or extensive prior experience to do PE. Simply follow the step-by-step approach, and you, too, can easily perform PE. This proven method enables you to provide meaningful data before and during training, rather than waiting until the end (as happens with most evaluation processes). Such a method provides a prediction (forecast) before training, allowing you to decide whether to train and allowing for just-in-time corrections during design, development, and delivery, thus enhancing the value of the training and providing, overall, a much better return on training dollars.

The primary audiences for PE are corporate training and development (T&D) and human resource development (HRD) professionals who have responsibility for training within their companies. There are several ways in which PE could be used:

- To predict financial benefits of training
- To document the merit and worth of training
- To set metrics (i.e., to predict) training success in relation to Intention (motivation to use back on the job), Adoption (application or transfer to the job), and Impact (tangible organizational results)
- To collect data and assess achievement against success metrics
- To establish a continuous improvement cycle to ensure that future deliveries maximize value
- To develop PE Dashboards for use in reporting to management and sponsors
- To use Intention results as lead indicators to Adoption and Adoption results as lead indicators to Impact; implement corrective actions during training to ensure that maximum results are realized

Another audience is business executives, many of whom believe that T&D and HRD should be held to the same performance standards as, for example, Marketing, Sales, Research and Development, Manufacturing, and Product Development. The PE approach is very attractive to those executives who want to know specifically what business results and organizational impact a training investment can be expected to provide. Think about PE as a form of business forecast that predicts the future as accurately as possible, given all the information available, including historical data and knowledge of any future events that might impact the forecast.

PE not only forecasts value, but it is also a monitor and control mechanism that involves three stages. The first stage is focusing on the right metrics for evaluating training. You could monitor many things, but you want to focus on those that impact the business. PE suggests measuring Intention, Adoption, and Impact.

The second stage is implementing steering control. When you're thinking about performance and you're in an operating period that starts on, say, January 1 and ends on December 31, you don't want to wait until December 31 to figure out that you've got a problem and then make some changes; you want to solve that problem as early as you can, by using PE results. As steering controls, Intention data are leading indicators to Adoption, and Adoption data are leading indicators to Impact. It's just like steering: we make changes when we know we've got a problem.

The third stage is using the right performance measures. We need to make sure that we've got appropriate measures by predicting training's Intention, Adoption, and Impact before we train.

The book is written for all for-profit organizations, and particularly for corporations; however, not only is it for small businesses that want a cost-effective way to evaluate training, it is also written for not-for-profit organizations, consultants undertaking corporate training evaluation, the military, and government agencies evaluating their own internal programs.

The principles in which PE is founded are evident throughout the book, and you should attempt to trace them whenever you can. But feel free to explore—to take the concepts, the tasks, and the outputs and make them your own. This book provides a step-by-step approach; follow it, but add your own ideas and spins to make it work for you in your own organization.

Dave Basarab
Suwannee, Georgia
December 2010

Introduction: An Innovative Method of Training Evaluation

I have been fascinated for years by the evaluation and measurement of training. In the 1980s, I launched a global evaluation system for NCR Corporation based on Don Kirkpatrick's four levels of evaluation. I had come from designing, developing, and delivering customer training and was asked to lead the company's training evaluation efforts. I agreed to do it, not even knowing what training evaluation was—a scary thought! And as I read and researched evaluation, I finally got my hands on Don's four evaluation levels. I thought, "Wow, this is great stuff—I think I can do this." Don launched his approach to evaluation in 1959, based on the assessment of training according to four levels of activity. I implemented all four levels on a variety of courses (sales training, leadership, systems engineering, and customer education). The philosophy I used was not that of proving the worth of training, but of improving training. On numerous occasions, outside corporations paid visits to benchmark my training evaluation system. I was proud to be an implementer of Don's work.

A few years later, as manager of evaluation for Motorola University, I was able to expand my evaluation to a broader audience, integrating it into the university's culture and way of doing business. I remember talking to Don numerous times; he shared with me that I was the first to truly implement his ideas on a global scale. At that time, under the leadership of Bill Wiggenhorn, Motorola University was considered the world's premier corporate university; with Bill's support, my training evaluation efforts began to evolve by using Motorola's Six Sigma approach to quality improvement. Using the company's Six Steps to Six Sigma program (I still have the course material, thirty years later, and I use the concepts to this day) and Don's approach, I launched a worldwide training evaluation system comprising the following:

- A Level 1 Reaction system with an end-of-course survey automated by scanning results, producing reports, setting standards for acceptable results (my first training evaluation predictions, by the way), and monthly review by each training region, which led to continuous improvement actions.

- A Level 2 Learning system that integrated testing (pretest, posttest, skill observation testing) into selected courses—we scanned results and produced quality achievement reports and management reviews to improve mastery results.

- A Level 3 Behavior system was developed and implemented by a cross-functional team of very talented people from Motorola University and its business units. We evaluated behavior transfer on dozen of courses, some global and some smaller region-specific or business-specific. We used the same credo: we were evaluating to improve results, not to prove how good we were. We integrated Six Sigma methods into data collection and analysis, which led to the offering of more classes for successful programs, the implementation of actions to improve results on marginal programs, and, in a few instances, the halting of training that was not delivering on-the-job results.

Time and time again, our training evaluation system was benchmarked. I was able to sell our evaluation services to other Fortune 500 companies, and I used the funds to enhance the university's evaluation system; I had moved from an implementer of Don's approach to an innovator.

After my time at Motorola, I ran the sales education team at Pitney Bowes, and we implemented Rob Brinkerhoff's High Impact Learning (2001) and Success Case Method (2005). This was good stuff. We were creating High Impact Learning Maps and using them to gain approval to proceed with training (our very first predictions of potential value). The maps were inputs to instructional design, development, delivery (classroom and online), and finally evaluation. We performed over a dozen success case studies, which led to improvements not only in our training offerings, but also in how the company supported participants post-training. More important, they demonstrated the true value that the training department was contributing to Pitney Bowes.

Like many heads of learning organizations, I based the personal performance ratings of myself and my team on (1) the number of participants trained, (2) the money expended (the expense), and (3) Level 1 end-of-course scores (aiming at 4.5 out of 5.0). When I implemented other training evaluation efforts, they ended up being lag indicators that showed results after training but that had little chance for improving our courses beyond design tweaks or instructor coaching. Basically: *Look how good we have been—can we have more budget next year?* The answer was usually *no*.

I remember Rob's sitting in my office one day as I struggled preparing next year's training strategy and budget. How could I show what value we would bring the following year beyond merely the number of employees trained and the amount of money spent? At Rob's suggestion, I developed a High Impact

Learning map for that year's training strategy and budget. It was three pages long—when in the past I had produced strategy/budget documents twenty to thirty pages long or longer. Armed with my "new and improved" strategy, I headed off to the annual strategic planning summit. I presented the strategy, along with my budget request. All seemed to go well, but those who have experience in corporate training know that budget approvals take months. I waited, hoping to get the funds I felt were needed if the training department were to be able to deliver the value we promised. And I was shocked when the final budget came back: all that I asked for, with another 25 percent added! This *was* good stuff.

Running Training as a Business

What really hit home was how I ran my training business in comparison to how my peers—the heads of Marketing, Research and Development, Manufacturing, Sales—ran their businesses. They created business cases that showed the return on their annual budgets; they predicted what the results would be. In fact, their performance reviews, merit increases, bonuses—indeed, their career success—hinged on their meeting predictions and creating shareholder value.

Why couldn't we do that in training? Predict value, measure against those predictions, use lead indicators to stay on track, report in a business format that executives could easily understand. We needed a method of assessing the business value of training, a method that would be straightforward to implement and that would be understandable and compelling to business leaders. We needed a method that would interweave outcomes and leading indicators into training during design and delivery—to move from an event-driven function to one that predicted success, that measured performance against those predictions, and that was seen as returning significant shareholder value for the funds invested.

Over the next few years, in various training leadership roles, I wrestled with this question but was unable to arrive at a suitable solution. Then, one day, I was at a senior executive summit during which the CEO announced, "In January, we were profitable by $81 million but missed our profit goal by $8 million." Normally, I would have been excited, would have begun to think about how my training function could help make up such a shortfall. But that day, I didn't care. In fact, I wrote I DON'T CARE in my journal.

I *didn't* care. A few days later, I was in my boss's office, showing her my journal. It wasn't her or the company, I told her: It was me. My passion was gone. A few months later, I retired from corporate life.

A New Beginning

I set out on my own as a consultant and (maybe) an innovator. I did a lot of teaching and consulting, but my thoughts kept coming back to running training like any other business function. I knew evaluation; I knew how to run a business. Could I combine the two and come up with a new and innovative approach? Slowly, the concepts of PE began to come to me. I kept a journal in which I constantly refined the approach, adding to it bit by bit. Eventually, I thought I had a sound model, one that solved the problem I was wrestling with: what I had come up with I called Predictive Evaluation (PE). And I was lucky: my first PE came from an existing client. Beginning with this first implementation, PE has evolved into what you read about in this book.

$18 Billion Transportation Company Uses PE

My client wanted to improve its safety record by reducing the number of safety incidents occurring in its engineering workforce (the men and women who built and maintained bridges, structures, and the like). Although its safety metrics were clearly in line with industry standards, the company was not satisfied; in fact, it wanted significant improvement. What was the vision of the vice president of engineering? "[O]ver time we take action which effectively reduces the at-risk behaviors and conditions causing injury to our employees."

The company had effective safety training, but management believed that leadership skills within its field leaders were necessary to eliminate all injuries. It launched an excellent, interactive two-day leadership program for 900+ leaders, and I was fortunate to be hired to be one of the facilitators/coaches delivering this course. The company tracked the usual things: (1) budget (it spent over $1 million), (2) the number of participants trained, and (3) end-of-course reaction scores.

After we had delivered the course, we debriefed with engineering executives, who had anecdotal evidence that the program was good, but who had no indication of the value delivered. Was it making a difference? Were leaders performing as hoped? What had it done to improve safety?

In the next year, the company wanted to expand the course to 3,000+ foremen; representatives asked me, "Dave, how are we going to know this is working?" I shared my PE approach with them, and they agreed that it was exactly what they were looking for.

The First Predictive Evaluation

I partnered with Dr. Marguerite Foxon (a colleague from my Motorola University days), and we implemented PE for the company. The undertaking was massive: twelve to eighteen courses per month, averaging twenty to twenty-five participants per class, over a ten-month period. So what did we do?

To start, we worked with a training steering committee (a group of sixteen leaders from the home office and the field) to predict Intentions (goals), Adoption, and Impact and to built a project plan for implementing the evaluation. During a one-day meeting, the committee reviewed the instructional design documents and then defined the goals that participants should author during the course and the beliefs expected to have been inculcated by course completion. We defined these as the course *Intentions*. Next we asked ourselves, *If the participants believe [the belief statements] and plan to do [the desired goals], how would that manifest itself in real work back on the job?* Answers to that question produced a list of desired behaviors the company required as expected performance. These became the course *Adoptions*. We then defined the results of the Adoptions (the expected results when participants successfully performed the desired work) and, finally, the business results from that adoption. We called this the course's *Impact* on the business—tangible value the training was forecast to deliver to the company.

As the final element in predicting the value of this training, the committee established "success gates" for Intention, Adoption, and Impact results. (A success gate sets the minimum results that are needed to claim the training as successful.)

The end result of the committee's efforts was an Impact Matrix for the course—a chart that showed alignment of course design to Intentions, Adoption, and Impact. This matrix was validated with 700 employees from the target population, as well as with twenty-four external facilitators who had taught the course the previous year. The committee reviewed the results and finalized the predictions with senior leaders. The Impact Matrix then became an input source for the instructional designer, who modified the course design and subsequent course materials.

We incorporated goal planning and data collection for each participant into the course. As participants completed the course, they created their own personal transfer plan by authoring a personal goal statement and telling us how they felt about the course beliefs. The goals were sent to us (the evaluators), and we entered them into a database and read every goal (approximately 5,500 during the year) to judge whether it met the criteria for an acceptable goal.

We delivered monthly Intention Dashboards to management to show whether or not the success gate for Intentions had been achieved. After closely monitoring Intention data for two months, we observed that some coaches (external facilitators) were allowing poor-quality goals to be written; this caused monthly Intention Scores to fall below the predicted success gate. After we held a session with the coaches to get them on track, Intention results were spectacular.

We also conducted three Adoption (transfer to job) evaluations and found that the goal of 70 percent of goals being successfully implemented had been far exceeded. We also collected and analyzed environmental and organizational factors that enabled or inhibited adoption and found common causes for both.

Last, we conducted three Impact evaluations and proved that the adopted leadership behaviors significantly influenced safety (35 percent reduction in major safety incidents). We also uncovered an unexpected result—there was substantial evidence that the leadership skills were helping shape a new culture within the company: one of collaborative, open communication, of being one's brother's (or sister's) keeper.

As a result, the company used PE (1) to document the course's value (impact) for safety and (2) to improve course design, delivery, transfer, and business results. Senior management was delighted with results and felt that it truly understood the contribution of training to improved safety outcomes—so much so that the course was fully funded, indeed, expanded, for the next year. And we were contracted to continue with PE.

I share with you a different approach to training evaluation, one built on the works of Don and Jim Kirkpatrick and Rob Brinkerhoff, with the addition of my new methods. For twenty-five years, I have been evaluating training; I hope this simple approach ensures that your training delivers business and organizational results.

Chapter 1

The Predictive Evaluation Approach

ASTD Study Shows Training Evaluation Efforts Could Be Enhanced

"The Value of Evaluation: Making Training Evaluations More Effective," an ASTD Research Study in 2009, shows that companies struggle with evaluating whether their programs meet the business needs of their organizations and whether they are meaningful to employees and business leaders. It also points out that the Kirkpatrick model is the most utilized evaluation approach followed by Brinkerhoff's success case method. Jack Phillips ROI (return on investment) model is also being employed. I was not surprised when in the report they stated that "The least likely metric is actual business outcomes, which nearly a quarter of respondents said they do not measure at all."[1]

You may wonder why they don't measure business outcomes. The report states that the following are most common barriers:

1. It is too difficult to isolate training's impact on results versus the impact of other factors.

2. Evaluation is not standardized enough to compare well across functions.

It paints an interesting picture of training evaluation in the United States, does it not?

What it tells me is that training evaluation's time has come, and it needs to be implemented like any of the other business measurement functions (Marketing, Finance, Customer Loyalty, and Service Quality). That is, sound business practices dictate that training collect data to judge progress toward meeting the organization's strategies and annual/multi-year operating plans. Predict (forecast) training's contribution to those plans. Collect data early and often with defined success gates, and implement mid-course corrections to address discrepancies and take advantage of new insights and opportunities. A company might make a mid-course correction because something is working very well and deserves more effort or resources.

Although current efforts to evaluate the impact of training do provide data, these data usually offer little insight on what corrections are needed in order to meet goals.

Predictive Evaluation: A New Approach

Predictive Evaluation (PE) is a new approach that provides compelling training data to executives, including (1) predicting success of training in the three areas of Intention, Adoption, and Impact and measuring to see if success has been achieved; (2) leading indicators of future adoption (transfer of learning) and Impact (business results); and (3) making recommendations for continuous improvement. PE has two major components: *predicting,* which is before-the-fact, to decide whether to train, and *evaluating,* which is an after-the-fact measurement against the predictions. The beauty of PE is that it uses leading measures (Intention and Adoption) as a signal of results (Impact). If the leading indicators are below predicted success gates, actions can be implemented to "right-the-ship" so that the desired results are realized.

Predictive Evaluation Benefits

What are the benefits of PE? You now can predict (forecast) training's value to the company, measure against those predictions, use leading indicators to ensure that you are on track, and report in a business format that executives easily understand. You can interweave outcomes and leading indicators into training during the design and delivery and move from an event-driven function to one that predicts success, measures its performance against those predictions, and is seen as returning significant shareholder value for the funds invested.

However, the greatest strength of the PE approach is not about how it is communicated to the executives, or the tools, or the results, but rather how it requires participation of the supervisors and the employees in setting their *own* intentions and measurement of adoption. The approach treats the employees as adults owning their learning versus students checking off a class from their list and being measured by someone else.

The key components of the approach are the training program, training outcomes, prediction of value, Intention (to use), Adoption (actual use), and Impact (the results to the company). The following sections provide an overview of the approach and each of its key components. Detailed descriptions and guidance are given in Chapters 2, 3, 4, and 5.

Where to Start

The PE approach starts with an existing training program or one that is on the drawing board. In other words, PE works for both existing courses and new ones in the production queue. PE is independent of course delivery—it works equally well for classroom-based training, on-the-job training, online learning, simulations, workshops, etc. The approach works with different content—PE has been conducted on Leadership Training, Sales Training, Business Management Training, and Basic Management Training. PE is also independent of audience and has been used for groups from senior executives to hourly employees. Finally, PE can be employed for courses that are developed and delivered in-house (those where the company has internal personnel create and deliver the training) or outsourced courses (those purchased from external vendors to meet a company's training need).

To begin a PE on an existing course, you need to obtain and review instructional design documents (if they were created), course materials (participant and instructor), any existing evaluation data (such as Level 1 evaluation survey results), budget (actual expenses and projected expenses), number and types of employees already trained, and the number of employees who need training in the future. This is only the starting point—you can gather other information, such as opinions from participants, their supervisors, suppliers, instructors, and executives who sponsor the training. The purpose is to thoroughly understand and describe the object being evaluated (the training course). Once you understand the course. you can begin the predictive portion of PE.

But the best place to start a PE is on a course that is still on the drawing board. You don't start PE with the instructional design process, but it comes in as a component to ensure that the training design creates the proper value the company needs. In many instructional design processes, *Evaluate* is the final stage of the process. PE starts before the course finalizes its design, using its predictive components, and is an input/requirement for the final training design.

Typically, the predictive portion of PE begins for new courses when analysis and design phases of design are completed. In the Analysis phase, the instructional problem is clarified, the instructional goals and objectives are established, and the learning environment and participant's existing knowledge and skills are identified. The design phase deals with learning objectives, assessment instruments, exercises, content, subject matter analysis, lesson planning, and media selection.

Whether the course to be evaluated currently exists or is still under design, the PE approach makes the assumption that training programs are designed to provide participants with the following benefits:

- Knowledge: either new knowledge or a refresher of current knowledge
- Skills: new or improved techniques for getting work done
- Beliefs: the idea that the participants and/or their company can benefit from using the new knowledge and skills

- Behaviors: on-the-job practices and habits that shift or are adopted to improve actions and thinking that impact the business

Predictive Evaluation Framework

So let's look at the framework and premise that PE is based on. Before, during, and when they leave training, participants have some level of motivation to use what they have learned. I refer to this as "intentions." Intentions can be strong or weak. On the basis of their intentions, participants "adopt" (apply) the new skills as part of their work behavior (routine). Adopted behaviors practiced over time (repetition) produce results (an "impact") for the business. The magnitude and value of the results are affected by all three factors: (1) Intention, (2) Adoption, and (3) Impact. Using this as a basis for mirroring employee learning and performance, you can predict Intention, Adoption, and, finally, Impact. But before doing that, you need to understand the three PE elements (Intention, Adoption, and Impact).

Intention Evaluation

An Intention Evaluation (IE) addresses the following question: *Are participant goals and beliefs upon course completion aligned with desired goals?* Intentions are the goals that participants wish to achieve using the knowledge and skills they learned in training and supported by their beliefs.[2] This is the first evaluation focus point, because there is little or no adoption or business impact if participants have little or no intent to use the training. Intention Evaluation involves judging participant-authored goals against a predefined standard. If participant goals meet the standard, those goals are labeled as acceptable. Goals that do not meet the standard are labeled as unacceptable.

An *Intention Success Gate,* which is the percentage of acceptable goals, is predicted (e.g., 90 percent). Intention data are collected from participants via a goal planning sheet during training and submitted, after course completion, to the evaluator, who judges each goal as acceptable or unacceptable. This in turn creates an Intention Score (percentage of goals judged acceptable). When the Intention Score exceeds the Success Gate, the course is deemed successful (in creating the proper Intentions). If the Intentions Score is below the gate, an analysis of why and what can be done to improve results is undertaken. Intention data are leading indicators to Adoption (transferring knowledge and skills from training to the job). When Intention Scores meet Success Gate standards, there is a higher likelihood that the goals will be adopted.

The following are some questions and things to consider about Intention goals.

- *Are these goals supposed to be based on the goals that are developed by the stakeholders or program owners?* Answer: yes.

- *Do the participants get to use those as a basis for developing their own goals?* Answer: it is a good idea to share sample goals with participants so that they see how to construct a good goal. It also may stir their thinking on what they want to do.

- *Why do they author their own? Why don't they just use the ones designed by the stakeholders and write the how of implementation in their area?* Answer: by authoring their goal in their own words, they are creating their personal action plan. This is a method of determining how committed they are to implement the skills necessary to drive Adoption, which leads to predicted Impact. If you give them the list of stakeholder goals, you are testing the ability to choose versus understanding what it takes to perform the work.

- *Can instructors help them with their goals?* Answer: absolutely. A best practice is having the participant draft the goal(s), have it reviewed by the instructor, and then finalize it. Some courses have participants share the goals with each other—giving and receiving feedback to make the goals better.

- *What if the goals they come up with are completely different than the designer's intentions?* Answer: some analysis needs to be conducted to determine why this has happened. Typical causes are (1) the course teaches the wrong thing, (2) the course does not teach it well enough, (3) the participant is not from the target population and would have difficulty writing a good goal, (4) the participants are weak goal writers. Once the causes are identified, corrective actions can be implemented to eliminate or greatly reduce them.

The following are a few examples of well-written Intention goals:

- Show a more positive attitude, because I tend to be a grump the first couple of hours in the morning. I will smile and thank my team for their input. I will also ask open-ended questions during our daily morning meeting. The outcome I expect is that my team members will be motivated/happy to do their work and feel that they have a sense of accomplishment.

- I will be more patient in everyday tasks and when working with my coworkers and other departments by being open to new ideas, asking open-ended questions, listening, and using a positive attitude. The outcome I expect is to have a fun work environment and to show people that it is great to speak up about concerns.

- Make sure that at least once a week I give the sales and the customer service teams a chance to hold a briefing. I will mentor them on how to hold a top-notch briefing and give them feedback. The outcome I expect is for them to become more involved and give input and to build their confidence, resulting in increased sales.

Belief Evaluation

Beliefs are defined as "the idea that the participants and/or their company will benefit from using the new knowledge and skills." Belief data are also captured during goal creation but need not need be associated with a specific goal. Beliefs are derived from the course design and/or content and are answers to the question—*What do our employees need to believe so that they successfully transfer training skills to the job?* The following are a few belief examples:

- When leading people, my attitude makes a difference.
- I have a voice and can make a difference.
- I own the customer experience.
- Values drive results.
- A fun workplace drives productivity.

Participant belief data are captured on the goal planning sheet by having participants rate how meaningful the beliefs are to them. Typically a 7-point semantic differential scale is used, where 1 = Meaningless and 7 = Meaningful. As with goals, a Success Gate for beliefs is predicted, for example, *90 percent of the participants will rate beliefs as "top box" (a 6 or 7 on the 7-point scale)*. If the Success Gate is achieved, the course is successful from a Belief Evaluation standpoint. If results are below the gate, the course is viewed as unsuccessful and investigation and/or corrective actions are undertaken.

When the Intentions Scores for *both goals and beliefs* meet their respective Success Gates, the entire course (for that delivery) is deemed as meeting Intention predictions: it is classified as successful. When *either* one of the two Success Gates (Intention or Beliefs) fails to be met, the course (for that delivery) is viewed as unsuccessful.

Corrective actions on Intention results include course redesign, instructor improvement, making sure participants are from the target population, etc. For the participants who just completed the course and whose goals are below standard, you can work with them one-on-one or in small groups to author the right goals. You can even have their supervisors meet with them to "beef up" the goals so that they are pointed in the proper direction (for performance and Adoption).

Adoption Evaluation

An Adoption Evaluation addresses the following question: *How much of the training has been implemented on the job and successfully integrated into the participant's work behavior?* An Adoption Evaluation analyzes participant performance (behaviors and actions that the employee has transferred to the job) and participant goal completion rate against a defined Adoption Success Gate (percentage of employees performing as predicted). A set of on-the-job adoptive behaviors is developed from the course design or material and from the Intention goal and belief statements. A few examples of adoption behaviors are the following:

- Model a positive attitude by relating to coworkers as to what is currently going on with their problems and reward their positive attitude.

- Provide positive feedback when contacting my employees and providing recognition on sales milestones.

- Obtain and enhance Voice of Customer (VOC) intelligence for existing and potential customers.

- Estimate revenue and operating income for the annual and long-range business plans.

In this case, you want to know if the Intention goals have been implemented and are sustainable in the workplace. We are evaluating employees who are reporting goal completion—those who have completed their goal or who have made significant progress toward completion *and* whose on-the-job performance is similar to the defined adoptive behaviors. An Adoption Evaluation is usually conducted two to three months after participants have completed training, giving them time to attempt, adjust, and finally adopt their new skills and knowledge. Adoption data are collected by surveying participants seeking their transfer to-the-job. Environmental factors that have enabled and inhibited Adoption are also collected along with the result (Impact) from the participant's new performance.

An Adoption Rate Success Gate is set (predicted) defining the percentage of participants who will successfully implement goals that are similar to the adoptive behaviors (performance on-the-job). An example of an Adoption Rate Success Gate is this: *60 percent of employees will have successfully implemented one or more of the adoptive course behaviors*. This is the target that the company expects from course participants. If the Success Gate is met, in terms of Adoption Evaluation, the training is deemed successful. If however, the Adoption Rate is below the Success Gate, root cause analysis is conducted, and corrective actions are put in place. These corrections can be for the group that has just been evaluated, to lift its adoption rate, and/or for future participants, to ensure that they adopt the right things at the right rate. Examples of corrective actions based upon Adoption Evaluation are the following:

- Review the inhibiting factors and attempt to minimize them. For example, if a large portion of the inhibitors resulted from lack of management support, you could (1) create a Job Aid for Managers, with tips for coaching and supporting their employees; (2) change the attendance policy and have managers attend with their employees; (3) require all managers to meet with their employees one week after graduation and build the use of the new skills into the employee's annual objectives.

- Maybe an inhibitor is pointing toward insufficient knowledge or skills to do the job correctly. In this case, you could (1) change course design and delivery to enhance the learning of that knowledge and skill; (2) pair low-performing participants with high-performing participants to job shadow and learn the correct application; (3) provide remedial training via job aids, podcasts, Web meetings; (4) have high-performing employees share their success stories with others—what they did, when they did it, and how they did it.

You can also use high-performing participants' success stories as examples of how training can be employed back on-the-job. These can be shared in training by instructors or, even better, bring the participants to share their stories personally. At times, you can have successful participants mentor new participants.

Impact Evaluation

An Impact Evaluation addresses the following questions: *What business results can be traced back to the goal adoption of participants? Are results to the business as predicted? What is the typical profile of a participant who has achieved results? What additional business results (value) could be achieved if participants who have little/no adoption were to adopt their goals?* An Impact Evaluation assesses the changes to organizational results attributable to the use of skills mastered in training.

Using the behaviors from the Adoption predictions, you determine the value from one person successfully performing the unit of work. Then, based on course design and business performance requirements (when the participant could and should do the work), you determine how frequently one person should perform the unit of work, based on target audience and work practices (e.g., strategic planning usually has a frequency of once a year; using a specific response protocol while working the customer support phones would offer numerous opportunities daily). By estimating the number of employees to be trained over the life span of the course, noting the Adoption rate of participants actually performing the correct work, and taking into account that internal and external factors working on the company contribute to the results, you can predict the Impact that the company should receive.

Participants identified in the Adoption Evaluation phase as those who have self-reported as achieving their goals are surveyed to capture further results and are then interviewed. Using this Impact data, profiles of participants whose use of the skills that have produced the greatest impact are developed, along with examination of company records to show actual value realized. This becomes the value realized for Impact Evaluation, and when actual results exceed the gate, the course is successful in delivering on its promised value. If values are below the gate, determining why results are below expectation leads to the necessary corrections (to the course, organizational support, etc).

Predicting the Value of Training

Now that you have a basic understanding of Intention; Adoption; and Impact Evaluation, let's look at predicting the value of training. Predicting training results is a similar method, which business executives use for deciding which equipment to purchase, what products to launch, whether or not to expand the workforce, etc. Lacking sufficient information, decision makers could fail to support those training programs that have the greatest potential for producing significant value to the company. When decision makers decide to spend large sums of money on training, they seek to evaluate their options as they evaluate other large investments—on the basis of financial returns to the company. This approach allows you to predict results prior to training delivery (early in the design process), decide whether the benefits (value gained) are worth the investment, and, if the choice is to train, evaluate and report so that corrective actions are implemented as needed.

PE allows you to predict what Impact (results) will be realized by your company, what behaviors will result in Adoptions (transfer) for participants and at what success rate, and what Intentions (goals and beliefs) participants must author, thereby enabling them to begin Adoption. Note: detailed instructions, steps, tools, and tips to predict are explained in *Chapter 2: Predicting Training's Value*.

Working with a team of subject matter experts, staff from various lines of business, Human Resource personnel, Finance personnel, instructional designers, target audience members, and performance technologists, you produce the course's Impact Matrix—the prediction of training value. The Impact Matrix documents the following for the course:

- Goals that participants should author during training and the Success Gate

- Beliefs that participants should have on course completion and the Success Gate

- Adoptive behavior and the Success Gate (Adoption rate)

- Frequency of adoption: how often the work is performed

- Results of performing the Adoptive behavior

- External contribution factor: the percentage that other influences beyond training contribute to the results

- The predicted Impact that a set of participants will produce over time

Cost to design, develop, maintain, and evaluate the training is calculated for the course's life span. This, along with the Impact Matrix and course design document, are presented to key decision makers to aid in determining whether or not to move forward with the training investment. The PE predictions provide key decision makers with the following:

1. A clear picture of the business outcomes

2. Outcomes that can be classified and placed in order of importance with other non-training investment decisions

3. Alternatives that may be explored (e.g., different course design, scope of implementation, non-training solutions to the problem, etc.)

Companies typically follow a minimum rate of return or payback policy that provides guidance on whether the company should move forward with any large investment. This is usually provided by the Finance department, and the predicted Impact and budget are critical for making informed investment decisions.

Training's Merit and Worth

Adoption and Impact evaluation demonstrate the worth of the training program to business executives—by showing the progression of employees from course attendees to high-performing employees, to bottom line results that contribute to profitable growth. This element of the PE approach provides information in

Figure 1: Training's Merit and Worth

a continuous improvement cycle. Data from the first round of Adoption and Impact evaluation are used to enhance the likelihood of greater Adoption and greater Impact on future deliveries.

PE provides data on the merit and worth of training. Merit answers the question: *Does the training do what it is supposed to do?* Worth answers the question: *Does the course add value beyond itself?* (Figure 1)

Intention data, goals, and beliefs indicate whether the training is working during delivery. In other words, does the course (learning experience) create the right intentions in participants? This is considered the merit of the training. Adoption and Impact data are considered the worth of training because they show the value of the program after the learning event has concluded.

In summary, predicting training's value helps you understand the meaning and significance of key financial impact that your training provides to the company. It allows key decision makers to use financial analysis to maintain fiscal discipline and to make sound business decisions. It provides a roadmap, via training, to revenue and profit potential. And, last, it allows you to manage the training's overall performance and document its contribution to the company.

Why Predictive?

PE employs a business model that executives are used to. It provides metrics that executives and sponsors care about. It forces you to think through the outcomes beyond learning objectives and instructional design strategies. In fact, predicting results ensures that the course is aligned with creating business value. The predictions can aid in deciding whether the training investment should be funded. If the benefits (Impact) predicted are not attractive to company decision makers, the effort should be stopped. However, with solid prediction of value delivered, decision makers will approve the training effort. Clearly, PE should be included very early in the instructional design process. It reflects what everyone else in business—for example, product managers, Research and Development, Manufacturing, Marketing, Sales—has to do, and it is time that training had a method to do the same.

The PE Sequence

Now that you have an understanding of PE, you are ready to start. A typical PE sequence includes these steps:

1. Choose the course you wish to evaluate; it can be a new course design or a course that already exists.

2. Review the course to fully understand what it is, what it is supposed to teach, how participants learn the material, what business issues it addresses, who is to attend, how they attend, what pre-course preparations are in place, what post-course support mechanisms exist, who are the sponsors, what sponsors see as the purpose for the course.

3. Form a committee to predict training value: create the Impact Matrix and present the predictions to key decision makers *(see Chapter 2: Predicting Training's Value)*.

4. Evaluate Intentions: during course pilot and for every session thereafter *(see Chapter 3: Intention Evaluation)*, improve results as necessary by conducting root cause analysis and implementing corrective action.

5. Evaluate Adoption: determine how often and when to conduct Adoption Evaluations *(see Chapter 4: Adoption Evaluation)*. Improve results as necessary by conducting root cause analysis and implementing corrective action.

6. Evaluate Impact: determine how often and when to conduct Impact Evaluations *(see Chapter 5: Impact Evaluation)*. Improve results as necessary by conducting root cause analysis and implementing corrective action.

How PE Differs from Other Approaches

Is PE for you? How is it different than other training evaluation approaches? PE is a new approach to training evaluation; see the following chart for a side-by-side comparison.

Typical Approach	PE
Focus on costs and numbers, not on forecasting financial return. Training groups rarely predict the value-add of their training to the company before the training is undertaken. At best, they provide information about costs, who and how many will be trained, and the training schedule. As a result, management views training in cost and activity terms, not in terms of its financial value to the organization.	**Focuses on the predicted impact and its value-add to the organization.** Integrated with instruction design activities, PE enables the training function to forecast (predict) the quantifiable impact of training. This allows management to judge potential training investments in terms of predicted business results and value returned.
Evaluation is after-the-fact, with no measures of success. Most training functions rely on the "Levels" approach. Although most do an end-of-course evaluation ("Happy Sheet"), relatively few evaluate transfer or impact on business results. Those that do, perform evaluation at the completion of training, thus leaving little or no opportunity to improve the results.	**Employs repeated measures that mirror employees' path to improved performance with predicted Success Gates.** PE provides management with high-value training data, including (1) predictions of success in the three areas of Intention, Adoption, and Impact; (2) leading indicators of future adoption (transfer of learning); (3) business dashboards showing Impact (return on investment in the form of business results); and (4) recommendations for continuous improvement while training is being delivered.
ROI and/or Cost-Benefit evaluation. ROI evaluation, when it is attempted by trainers, often overrelies on subjective estimates of the percentage of return. An ROI figure has little value for making decisions about the program. Cost-benefit evaluation requires significant use of statistics to provide useful data. Both types of evaluation are conducted well after training has concluded and do not provide data that can be used to improve the program in real time.	**Provides concrete, business-focused, and evidence-based data on return on investment.** Data collection is robust and rigorous, and management finds the data far more compelling, convincing, and useful.

Typical Approach	PE
Existing approaches work after the fact with one-off programs. Data are not collected until program completion, allowing no opportunity for midcourse correction or feedback.	**Works well with programs that have repeated deliveries over time.** PE offers a carefully determined prediction of the extent of transfer and impact. PE identifies the expected outcomes, assesses progress against those at regular intervals during the delivery time frame, and provides feedback that can be used to make changes, mid-course corrections, etc., both in relation to the program and to the application environment.

Good luck and happy evaluating!

Chapter 2

Predicting Training's Value

Business forecasting is indeed big business, with companies investing tremendous resources—in systems, time, and employees—aimed at bringing useful projections into the planning process. Business forecasting is a process used to estimate or predict future patterns using business data. Some examples of business forecasting include estimating quarterly sales, product demand, customer lifetime value and churn potential, inventory and supply-chain reorder timing, workforce attrition, and Web site traffic and predicting exposure to fraud and risk. Basically business forecasting is used to try to predict the future.

When we *predict training's value,* we are using a form of business forecasting—estimating what training will deliver in terms of increased organizational and business results. These predictions come in the form of participant Intentions, Adoption, resulting Impact on the business, and the costs to deliver the value. These predictions enable decision makers to make highly informed proactive decisions. As with any business forecasting method, predicting training's value has benefits and drawbacks that need to be weighed before proceeding.

The *benefits* of predicting training's value are that it aids in decision making (should a business move forward with the training or not); it provides input to decisions about planning and resource allocation (people and budgets); and if data are of high quality, it can create an accurate picture of the future. Its *drawbacks* are that data are not always reliable or accurate; data may be out of date; qualitative data may be influenced by peer pressure; and difficulty of coping with changes to external factors may be out of the business's control— for example, economic policy, competition, political developments, and natural disasters—hurricanes, earthquakes, etc. Predicting training's value involves the following steps:

- Step 1: Identify and completely understand the course to be evaluated.
- Step 2: Form a steering committee to develop the predictions.
- Step 3: Create the course's *Impact Matrix*—this is the prediction of training's value.
- Step 4: Validate the matrix with sponsors, intended participants (the target audience), and the Finance organization. Note: some companies have a Strategic Planning/Forecasting department, and it needs

to be represented on the steering committee or at least included in the validation process.

- Step 5: Finalize the matrix.
- Step 6: Present the Impact Matrix to key decision makers for approval to move forward with the training or not.

So when do you predict training's value? To start, you need to choose a course on which you want to perform a PE. That course (training) is in one of two states: it is a *new course* in the design phase or an *existing course* that you plan to continue (deliver in the future). Note: you may also have a course that is being redesigned. In any case, you want to predict future business results to aid the company in deciding to (1) move forward with the training because the predicted results are attractive, (2) use predictions to alter training design, or (3) decide not to train (cancel the instructional design or stop teaching the existing course). You are providing key decision makers with information so that they can weigh all the possibilities to make an informed decision on the training investment.

A word of caution—predicting training value is not a substitute for sound instructional design. It is in fact a valuable input into the design process. Most course design and development efforts use some version of the ADDIE model— a systematic instructional design process consisting of five phases: (1) Analysis, (2) Design, (3) Development, (4) Implementation, and (5) Evaluation. Figure 2 shows how to integrate PE into the ADDIE model. Note: the Evaluation section of the ADDIE model has been replaced with PE.

The first step in instructional design is the *Analysis* phase. During analysis, the designer identifies the learning problem, the goals and objectives, the

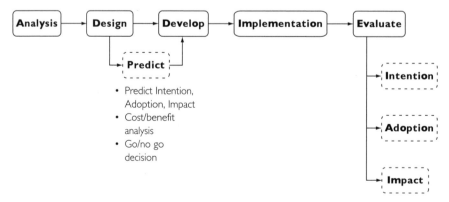

Figure 2: Integrating PE into the ADDIE Model

audience's needs, existing knowledge, and any other relevant characteristics. Analysis also considers the learning environment, any constraints, the delivery options, and the timeline for the project. All of these elements are input to the Design phase and the predicting activities.

The *Design* phase is the systematic process of specifying learning objectives. Detailed design documents are created to provide a blueprint for the development phase. With this, you have a solid idea of what the course is going to look like (classroom, online learning, workshop, agenda, target audience, length, learning activities, etc.).

During prediction efforts, the course design may need to change to ensure that training delivers the desired Intention, Adoption, and Impact. As the design changes, predictions may be modified so that there is direct alignment between course design and predictions. This cycle repeats until the Steering Committee and the designer are satisfied. The PE output of this work is the Impact Matrix, which documents predicted value. The matrix is presented to key decision makers as the forecast of training return; then, using this information, they decide whether to move forward with the training efforts. Using the Impact Matrix, they know what they are investing in, who will be trained over what period, the new performance that their employees will have, results the new performance will deliver, and the cost (investment) to achieve this.

If you have built your training business case well and it is approved, the *Develop* phase of instructional design begins. This entails the actual creation (production) of the content and learning materials based on the Design phase. In other words, the course is created based on the design specification and in alignment with the predictions.

After the course is developed, instructional design's *Implementation* phase is performed. During implementation, the program is launched and procedures for training the participant and instructors are implemented. Implementation usually starts with a pilot or a series of pilots to test the course, review results, and modify the course as needed. During the pilot period, you collect Intention data (goals and beliefs), judge them, and calculate the Intention Score. The Intention results, along with Level 1 survey results and the instructional designer's observation, form the basis for determining what changes are needed and whether the course is ready for full implementation.

After pilot, ongoing delivery takes place—with Intention, Adoption, and Impact evaluations being conducted as planned.

For more information on ADDIE, see the following:

- Dick, W., & Carey, L. (1996). The Systematic Design of Instruction (4th Ed.). New York: Harper Collins College Publishers. 7th edition, 2008.

- Leshin, C. B., Pollock, J., & Reigeluth, C. M. (1992). Instructional Design Strategies and Tactics. Englewood Cliffs, NJ: Education Technology Publications. 7th edition (2008)

How to Predict Training's Value

Okay, you are probably saying to yourself, I get that, but how do I predict? Good question. The rest of this chapter takes you through the steps to do just that. To help you understand the prediction procedures, worked PE examples from *Business Acumen Training* (BAT) are provided. BAT is a four-day business management course for a Fortune 50 global company that I had the honor to evaluate. You will learn the tasks, tips, and techniques to predict, and you can follow along with the examples. So let's get predicting!

Step 1: Identify and Completely Understand the Course to Be Evaluated

Predicting activities are initiated when someone has chosen that a specific training program requires an evaluation, or at least the predictive portion. Remember that the training can be a new course being designed or an existing course. To predict and eventually evaluate a course, you need to understand it thoroughly. You need to answer as many of the following questions as possible. This helps you collect enough information about the course so that you can develop its predictions.

- What is the name of the course?
- How will it be delivered?
- How long is it?
- What is the definition of the training need?
- Who will be trained?
- What is the life span for the course?
- How many employees will be trained per year?
- When will it start?
- Who is doing the design?
- Who will be doing the development?
- Who will be delivering the training?
- What are the desired outcomes from the course, stated in business terms?
- What are the desired performance standards for participants?

- Who are the sponsors?
- Who are the stakeholders?
- What is the outline/agenda for the course?
- What are the learning objectives?

These data are collected from a variety of sources, such as instructional design documents, existing course materials, sponsors, stakeholders, past or future participants, key business leaders, Human Resource professionals, etc. This is only the starting point for course information. The more data you collect, the better your predictions will be. You may add as many other questions and answers as you like.

Step 2: Form a Steering Committee to Develop the Predictions

As soon as you have adequate information to describe the course, establish a Steering Committee of eight to twelve people to develop the predictions. Ideally, this group is made up of individuals from the learning function along with subject matter experts from business units and functional units; it may also include external consultants. Ideally, they are people who represent their function or business unit and have the expertise to provide valuable insight during the prediction process.

The initial role of the Steering Committee is to create the course's Impact Matrix—essentially the forecast of value from training. Together, Steering Committee members make the detailed decisions about the predictions and about which other individuals or units to involve in data gathering and decision making, validating the predictions, and championing the predictions. Once the Steering Committee has created the Impact Matrix and the decision to move forward with training has been made, committee members take on the role of reviewing PE Dashboards (reports) and, when appropriate, taking action to correct problems.

There is one additional role that merits being mentioned, which is you, as the evaluator. Your responsibility during predicting is that of facilitator and evaluation expert. You are not a decision maker on Impact Matrix content and predictions. You facilitate working sessions, run the process, assemble the committee's draft and final documents, and provide expert advice on evaluation.

Step 3: Create the Course's *Impact Matrix*

The best way to develop training predictions is to bring the Steering Committee together to create the Impact Matrix. This is usually done in one of two ways:

a face-to-face meeting (usually one day)—with you, the evaluator, facilitating the session or a series of virtual meetings (i.e., Web meetings), again, with you facilitating. Who should attend these meetings? The meeting attendees should be the Steering Committee, an executive sponsor (person who has charted the team and/or the training), instructional designer, external providers/consultants, and other training personnel as needed. A typical agenda for the prediction meeting is the following:

Agenda Item	Comments
Opening Comments: Executive Sponsor	Charters the team to develop the predictions, sets stage for the importance of accurate forecasting, ties the effort in to annual company forecasting efforts, discusses what happens after the Impact Matrix is created
The Course: Instructional Designer (or training professional)	Presents course information so that Steering Committee has a thorough understanding of the training
The Impact Matrix: Evaluator	To fulfill their role, members of the Steering Committee need to understand the concept of the Impact Matrix—what it is, how they will create it, how it is used, etc.
Ground Rules: The Committee	Team ground rules define how individuals treat each other, communicate, participate, cooperate, support each other, and coordinate joint activity. They are used to define and standardize team procedure, use of time, work assignments, meeting logistics, preparation, minutes, discussion, and decision making.
Create Impact Matrix: The Committee	The Impact Matrix builds one component at a time. Prediction items developed (in order) are Beliefs, Intention Goals, Adoptive Behavior, Adoption Rate, Results of Adoptive Behavior, Value of Results, External Contribution Factor, Training Cost, and Return-on-Investment.
Next Steps: Evaluator	Inform the Steering Committee of the next steps: validation of the Impact Matrix with others and then reconvening to review validation data and finalize the map.

Description of the Business Acumen Course

Because an actual Business Acumen course has been used in the worked examples, a brief description of that training is provided. The Course—*Business Acumen Training (BAT)* is a four-day classroom event created for a global Fortune 50 manufacturing firm. This course provides participants with the ability to grow the business, increase speed to market, lower costs, and enhance margins in all economic cycles and with an opportunity to learn and network with other company business leaders. The topics covered in BAT include the following:

- Strategy into Action
- Financial Analysis and Interpretation
- Assessing Business Opportunities
- In Pursuit of Legendary Customer Experiences
- Innovation and Creativity as Drivers of Strategic Change

Specifically, participants learned how to do the following:

- Become more customer centric
- Establish business principles that are consistent and repeatable
- Develop more astute business leaders across the enterprise
- Enhance leadership decision making
- Increase revenue through innovation and recurring revenue
- Effectively contribute to the company's financial targets of: 8–12 percent Revenue Growth, 4–6 percent Organic Growth, 4–6 percent Growth via Acquisitions, 15 percent Operating Margin, 12–15 percent EPS Growth, and 15 percent Return on Invested Capital (ROIC)

The target audience for BAT is an employee who manages managers. The total potential population (in role and high-potential employees) is approximately 1,500 employees. This course primarily utilizes lecture, case study, and a business simulation exercise that is designed to be an interesting and engaging vehicle to maximize learning effectiveness for this content. The course is facilitated by four external faculty members and requires completion of pre-work.

Predict Beliefs

With the Steering Committee in place and having a good understanding of the course, you start by predicting beliefs—what you want the participants to believe in when they complete the course. You need to explain beliefs to the Committee.

Brian Tracy in his book *Goals! How to Get Everything You Want—Faster Than You Ever Thought Possible*[1] says this about beliefs: "Perhaps the most important of all mental laws is the Law of Belief. This law says that **whatever you believe with conviction becomes your reality.** You do not believe what you see; you see what you already believe. You actually view your world through a lens of beliefs, attitudes, prejudices, and pre-conceived notions. You are not what you think you are, but what you think, you are."

I believe that when participants believe that new skills and knowledge mastered in training will help them and/or their organization, the likelihood of adoption is increased. When participants change their beliefs about themselves and their personal performance, they apply the new skills and even take on new challenges. Beliefs manifest themselves in words and actions. Therefore training should instill the set of beliefs that support participants in trying, practicing, and finally transferring these skills. You do not teach beliefs in training, but the design should develop the belief structure during the learning experience. The instructional design needs to make sure that everything that is said and done in the course is consistent with the training's belief statements. A few techniques include guest speakers sharing their success stories using the new skills, the language that instructors use when teaching, posters (signage) in the classroom, etc.

You start authoring belief statements by having the Committee answer this question: *Looking at the course and our company's culture and values, what beliefs do participants need so that they produce the desired business results?* Another way to stimulate creation of belief statements is with this question: *If participants from this course were the most competent and highly respected business leaders in the company, what would they believe in?*

Use silent brainstorming and affinity process techniques for developing the belief statements. These techniques are useful in gathering a lot of individual input in a short time. The steps are the following:

1. Have each member take five to ten minutes to generate silently as many belief statements as possible (answer to the question posed earlier) and record one answer per post-it note. Keeping the belief statements to fifteen to twenty words.

2. Each member then takes his or her ideas and posts them on a flip chart hanging on the wall. You should have dozens of belief statements on the flip chart.

3. Members then perform an Affinity Process by gathering all the belief statements that seem to be alike, discuss as a group how the cluster of statements are alike, and come up with a heading—the overarching belief statement. Allow fifteen to twenty minutes for the discussion.

There should be ten to twelve belief statements at this point. Note: the most important and meaningful conversations about beliefs happen at this time—be sure to allot enough time for this to occur.

4. In the context of the course, beliefs are not created equal. Therefore, the list of belief statements needs to be narrowed to the salient few (three to five) that drive adoption. Use a Priority Voting technique to accomplish this. Divide the number of belief statements (headers) by 3; the resulting number determines how many votes each member receives (dots or check marks that are used to vote). Each member then votes for the beliefs which he or she feel best answer the question posed at the beginning of the exercise. The statements with the highest votes become the beliefs for the course. Record these on a new flip chart and label it "Beliefs."

Note: A well-written Belief statement should complete the sentence: *I believe that* . . . . For the BAT, the Beliefs were the following:

- **B1**: Business leaders must operate with a customer-centric focus.

- **B2**: Customer intimacy is a transformative strategy that results in improved sales, service, and overall satisfaction.

- **B3**: Successful execution of strategy is a function of thinking, planning, action, and learning.

- **B4**: Use of appropriate metrics drive accountability and results.

- **B5**: Innovation is a key to sustainable and profitable growth.

Other belief examples include the following:

For a leadership course:
- Soft skills lead to hard results.
- A fun workplace drives productivity.
- Values drive results.
- Talented people who are properly developed (trained, coached, rotated, etc.) are successful.
- Synergy and collaboration create value in organizations and are worth the cost and energy.
- Interdependencies produce success.
- Employees are integral to our company's success.

For sales training:
- Territory Management increases the number of customers in the sales pipeline.

- Communicating the value of our organization's offerings differentiates us from the competition.
- Need-Based Dialogue accurately discovers a client's full range of needs.
- Addressing the sub-book and secondary conversations can make or break a complex sale.
- Passion is an effective sales tool.
- Complex sales are never won or lost on price alone.
- Solution selling significantly improves the odds of winning complex sales opportunities.

The belief statements are the first element of the Impact Matrix and are expressions of the desired set of feelings and attitudes participants need to transfer skills to their jobs successfully.

Predict Intention Goals

PE Intention Goals are the planned actions that we want participants to author during training as their personal transfer plan. If training is working as designed, we want participants writing actions that drive desired adoptive behaviors back into their everyday work patterns. Developing Intention Goals is relatively easy if the course has a set of well-written, performance-based learning objectives. They refer to training outcomes that specify the information and/or skills to be mastered and what participants do to demonstrate mastery. Performance-based learning objectives manifest themselves in training in the forms of content modules and skill-practice exercises. Therefore, the path to developing Intention Goals is performance-based learning objectives, which lead to course content/learning, which leads to Intention Goals. To create Intention Goals, you review the performance-based learning objectives and the course content/learning and answer two questions:

1. *In what work **situations** do we want participants to apply the learned content?*

2. *In those situations, what **observable actions** (work) will they do?*

For example, if a performance-based learning objective for a Foundational Management course is "Conduct highly interactive weekly staff meetings using open-ended and probing questioning techniques" and the instructional design calls for a twenty-minute lecture on open-ended and probing questions, with three fifteen-minute practice sessions running a meeting using the questioning techniques, the Intention Goal could be "During my weekly staff meeting, I will ask three open-ended and probing questions. I will involve all of the team and not just the supervisors."

Instructional Design		Intention Goal	
Performance-based learning objective	Course content/learning that teaches the objective	In what work **situations** do we want participants to apply the learned content?	In those situations, what **observable actions** (work) will they do?
(A)	(B)	(C)	(D)

Figure 3: Intention Goal Worksheet

A tool that you can use with the Steering Committee to develop these goal statements is the Intention Goal Worksheet (Figure 3).

In Column A, pre-populate the worksheet with the performance-based learning objectives that you feel warrant an Intention Goal. A good rule of thumb to determine which objectives to include on the worksheet is: include the terminal course objectives versus enabling objectives. Terminal objectives describe the participant's expected level of performance by the end of the course/training and describe results, not processes. Terminal objectives assist in focusing efforts and developing enabling objectives. Enabling Objectives define the skills, knowledge, or behaviors that participants must reach in order to complete terminal objectives successfully. Note: I use the term "performance-based learning objectives" with Steering Committee members because committee members are not instructional designers and grasp the meaning of that phrase better than using "terminal objectives."

In Column B, list the learning activities in the course design that teach the terminal objectives. These are the lessons, exercises, games, activities, etc. that participants experience to master the terminal objective. These are also pre-populated from the training design.

The Steering Committee completes Columns C and D. The steps to develop Intention Goals using the worksheet are the following:

1. Analyze the instructional design and determine the number of performance-based learning objectives you feel warrant an Intention Goal. Divide that number by 3; the result is the number of sub-teams you form from Steering Committee members.

2. Each sub-team has a worksheet with one to three performance-based learning objectives with Columns A and B filled out. Note: each sub-team has a unique set of objectives to work with.

3. Assign members to a sub-team (it is a good idea to do your best to have a diverse set of functions and expertise represented on each team) and give them their worksheet.

4. For each row, the teams read worksheet Columns A and B and complete Columns C and D. Note: sometimes an example (a completed row—Columns A to D) is included on the worksheet to provide members with a sample of the desired work output. Provide twenty to thirty minutes for sub-teams to complete their work. Have them post their draft worksheets on a flip chart.

5. Because sub-teams have worked independently from the other teams, they need feedback on their draft goals. There are two simple ways to gather feedback:

   a. The Museum Walk: in this approach, teams walk around the room and read the other team's work and, on a blank flip chart, provide suggested changes, items to add or delete, or any other useful comments.

   b. The Short Presentation: each team presents its draft goals to the larger group, soliciting suggestions for improvement and comments.

6. Teams take the feedback and finalize their Intention Goals.

7. Transfer all the goals to a central flip chart so that the Sub-Committee can vote on those that will be part of the Impact Matrix.

8. You may use the dot voting technique described earlier, or some other method of deciding on the Intention Goals. Another voting technique is Negative Voting,[2] which identifies which members do *not* support a goal instead of those who do. How do you use Negative Voting?

   a. Ask the members this question: *Who cannot live with this goal?* Count and chart the number of people who raise their hands. Do this for each proposed goal.

   b. Obtain permission from the Committee to eliminate the goals with the highest number of negative votes.

   c. Taking the remaining goals one at a time, ask each dissenting voter what concerns he or she has about that goal. Chart these concerns.

   d. When finished, ask the entire group to brainstorm ideas that eliminate the listed concerns.

e. After you have finished brainstorming, ask "dissenters" if the Committee's suggested changes allow them to support the goal.

f. Do a second negative vote. *Who cannot support goal 1 when it includes these changes?* If concerns still exist, repeat steps C, D, and E for those goals. By this time, almost all objections should have been heard and addressed.

g. Follow up with a *positive vote* on each goal. Majority rules—these are the Intention Goals.

Transfer the Intention Goals to a flip chart and post it below the flip chart with the Beliefs on the wall. Figure 4 is one of the completed Intention Goal worksheets for BAT.

Instructional Design		Intention Goal	
Performance-based learning objective	*Course content/learning that teaches the objective*	*In what work* **situations** *do we want participants to apply the learned content?*	*In those situations, what* **observable actions** *(work) will they do?*
(A)	(B)	(C)	(D)
Attain and enhance Voice of Customer (VOC)—convert customer knowledge into game-changing ideas.	**In Pursuit of Legendary Customer Experiences** This module focused on building a framework for customer intimacy to leverage the firm's existing customer base as well as attract and retain the right customers. Participants learned specific voice of the customer (VOC) methods applicable to the company then focused on converting deep customer insight from VOC into actions that create legendary customer experiences.	• Annual business unit strategic planning efforts • Annual customer loyalty assessments	• Conduct VOC in the form of market research, customer surveys (both potential and current customers), customer interviews and meetings, and focus groups with customers. • Synthesize and summarize VOC data into fundamental insights of customer needs that lead to products that provide superior value to the customer.

Figure 4: Business Acumen Intention Goal Worksheet Example

The complete set of Intention Goals for BAT was the following:

- **G1**: Annually, in strategic planning sessions or customer loyalty assessments, conduct Voice of Customer (VOC) research, synthesize, and summarize findings into fundamental insights of customer needs.

- **G2**: Within four weeks, establish milestones on progression in changing team's perspective to focus on recurring customer revenue rather than focusing exclusively on product.

- **G3**: Monthly, during budget and sales review, apply financial analysis to assess growth opportunities.

- **G4**: After the company's annual plan is finalized, translate enterprise strategies into your own strategy and annual operating plan.

You now have the first two components of an Impact Matrix. The next step is predicting the Adoptive Behaviors.

Predict Adoptive Behaviors

The Committee members must tackle the challenge of predicting the *Adoptive Behaviors* that they want participants to perform on-the-job. An Adoptive Behavior is the unit of work (what the participant does on-the-job, based on the intended goals, beliefs, and course design). The Adoptive Behaviors flow from the course design and are the manifestation of Intention Goals and Beliefs.

In predicting Adoptive Behaviors, Committee members answer this question: *If these are our best people at running a business, what work (behaviors) would the training with these goals and beliefs produce?* For example, recall the Intention Goal from the Foundational Management course: "During my weekly staff meeting, I will ask three open-ended and probing questions. I will involve all of the team and not just the supervisors." An Adoptive Behavior could be this: "Asked three open-ended and probing questions in staff meetings, conference calls, and one-on-one meetings with staff."

A tool that you can use with the Steering Committee to develop Adoptive Behaviors is the Adoptive Behavior Worksheet (Figure 5).

If the instructional design, Intention Goals, and Beliefs are in alignment and well written, the Adoptive Behaviors simply flow from them and are written as behaviorally based statements that describe the activities, tasks, procedures, and work that participants should perform on-the-job. Another way to think of this is that an Adoptive Behavior is a description of a performance that you want participants to do in order to be considered competent.

Intention Goals and Beliefs ➡	Adoptive Behaviors
Intention Goals	*If these are our best people at running a business, what **work (behaviors)** would the training with these goals and beliefs produce?*
• **G1:**	• **AB1:**
• **G2:**	• **AB2:**
• **G3:**	• **AB3:**
• **G4:**	• **AB4:**
Beliefs	
• **B1:** • **B2:** • **B3:** • **B4:** • **B5:**	

Figure 5: Adoptive Behavior Worksheet

To predict Adoptive Behaviors, do the following:

1. Using sub-teams from the Steering Committee, assign each team the task of developing Adoptive Behaviors for one Intention Goal.

2. Each team takes its goal and develops the Adoption Behavior(s) associated with that goal. Instruct team members to take into account the Belief statements, performance-based learning objective(s), and course content as they draft the behaviors. Allow twenty to thirty minutes for this activity. Inform the teams of the elements that a good Adoptive Behavior statement should contain:

   a. Directly aligned with the performance-based learning objective(s), course content, Intention Goal, and support by Belief statement(s)

   b. Clearly stated in observable on-the-job performance

   c. Realistic and doable, based on the target population for the course

   d. Appropriately comprehensive

Intention Goals and Beliefs ➡	Adoptive Behaviors
Intention Goals	*If these are our best people at running a business, what **work (behaviors)** would the training with these goals and beliefs produce?*
• **G1:** Annually in strategic planning sessions or customer loyalty assessments conduct VOC research, synthesize, and summarize findings into fundamental insights of customer needs.	• **AB1:** Obtain and enhance VOC for existing and potential customers.
• **G2:** Within four weeks, establish milestones on progression in changing team's perspective to focus on recurring customer revenue rather than focusing exclusively on product.	• **AB2:** Develop products/services roadmaps aligned with the goals of the customer while maximizing recurring revenue opportunity.
• **G3:** Monthly during budget and sales review, apply financial analysis to assess growth opportunities.	• **AB3:** Facilitate sessions with their team, discussing with them the ways in which they help to improve key financial metrics.
• **G4:** After the company's annual plan is finalized, translate enterprise strategies into my own strategy and annual operating plan.	• **AB4:** Lay out planned activities and corresponding monetary resources for the fiscal year, including recurring annual expenses and nonrecurring investments in special projects.
Beliefs	
• **B1:** Business leaders must operate with a customer-centric focus. • **B2:** Customer intimacy is a transformative strategy that results in improved sales, service, and overall satisfaction. • **B3:** Successful execution of strategy is a function of thinking, planning, action, and learning. • **B4:** Use of appropriate metrics drive accountability and results. • **B5:** Innovation is a key to sustainable and profitable growth.	

Figure 6: Adoptive Behaviors for Business Acumen Training

3. Once the teams have completed their draft behaviors, have them share the draft with the other teams and solicit opinions and suggestions for improvement.

4. Teams review the feedback given and make final adjustments to the behaviors.

5. Use a voting technique to gain consensus for the predicted Adoptive Behaviors.

6. Record the behaviors on a flip chart and place the charts on the wall to the right of the Intention Goals and Beliefs.

Figure 6 is an example of the completed Adoptive Behaviors for BAT.

Predict Goal Distribution

In order to predict training value (discussed later in this chapter), you need to forecast how the Intention Goals will be distributed among participants. In other words, if twenty participants attend training, what percentage will author goal 1, goal 2, goal 3, etc.? The percentages need to sum to 100 percent. To predict goal distribution, do the following:

1. Ask the Steering Committee to answer the question: *What percentage of participants will choose goal 1?* As the Committee wrestles with the answer, you may provide the following guidance:

    a. Look at the instructional design and the time allotted for each goal. Is there a goal with more instruction time than others? For example, if in a course 45 percent of the total time is spent teaching knowledge and skills associated with goal 2, maybe the goal distribution for goal 2 should be close to 45 percent.

    b. Is there a goal for which the content or skill to implement it is more complex than for other goals? Participants usually write goals that are most easy for them to implement. Therefore, the goal that is least complex to implement may warrant a higher goal distribution percentage.

    c. Does a goal lend itself more naturally to the target audience? For example, if the target audience is sales professionals, they may author goals on sales calling techniques versus budget analysis.

2. Once the Committee agrees on the goal distribution for goal 1, record it next to the Intention Goal and repeat the process for the remaining goals.

3. Facilitate a discussion on all the percentages (goal distributions); then use the Committee's agreed-upon decision-making process to finalize the distributions.

Continuing with our BAT example, the goal distribution that the Committee agreed to was the following:

- G1: 30 percent
- G2: 40 percent
- G3: 20 percent
- G4: 10 percent

What this is saying is that if 100 participants are trained, 30 will author a goal similar to Intention Goal 1, which should lead to Adoptive Behavior 1.

Predict the Adoption Rate

Not every participant will adopt his or her goals. The question is what is an acceptable percentage of those who adopt? That is what the *Adoption Rate*

Adoptive Behaviors	Adoption Rate
	What percentage of participants with this Intention Goal will successfully perform the Adoptive Behavior?
• **AB1:**	
• **AB2:**	
• **AB3:**	
• **AB4:**	

Figure 7: Adoption Rate Worksheet

tries to do. It is the percentage of participants that we want to perform the work (Adoptive Behaviors) and is the prediction of successful transfer from training to the workplace. The Steering Committee needs to answer this question for each Intention Goal: *What percentage of participants with this Intention Goal will successfully perform the Adoptive Behavior?* A tool to aid the Committee is *Adoption Rate Worksheet* (Figure 7).

Note: this is a whole group activity (the entire Steering Committee instead of teams). To develop Adoption Rates, do the following:

1. Review each Adoptive Behavior (one at a time), pose the question, and record the answer (percentages) on a flip chart. Committees, at times, struggle with the dilemma of this question: *Is this the percentage based on what we hope it will be, or is it the realistic value?* The percentage is a combination of both, based on the Adoptive Behavior and the work environment. Demands of the job, pressures to perform, participant's current job not providing an opportunity to practice the skill, and lack of management support are just some of the factors that impede adoption. The Committee needs to recognize this and set expectations accordingly. When Committee members are unsure, I recommend that a good starting point is somewhere near 60 percent.

2. Facilitate the discussion, refer back to the Adoptive Behavior, discuss, and agree to a proposed adoption rate.

3. Before you finalize the rate, it is a good idea to test the level of support from each member so that any objections can be heard and addressed. A technique I use is "Fist-to-Five."[3] Use this technique when Committee members need to come to consensus on an adoption rate; ensure that everyone in the group can support the rate. They

don't all have to think it's the best rate, but they should all agree that they can live with it. To use this technique, do the following:

a. Restate the adoption rate that the members have proposed; have everyone prepare to show his or her level of support.

b. When asked, each member responds by showing a fist or a number of fingers that corresponds to his or her opinion. **Fist:** a no vote—a way to block consensus. I need to talk more on the proposal and require changes for it to pass. **One Finger:** I still need to discuss certain issues and suggest changes that should be made. **Two Fingers:** I am more comfortable with the proposal but would like to discuss some minor issues. **Three Fingers:** I'm not in total agreement but feel comfortable to let this decision or a proposal pass without further discussion. **Four Fingers:** I think it's a good idea/decision and will work for it. **Five Fingers:** It's a great idea, and I will be one of the leaders in implementing it.

c. If anyone holds up fewer than three fingers, that individual should be given the opportunity to state his or her objections, and the team

Intention Goals	Goal Distribution	Adoptive Behaviors	Adoption Rate
• **G1:** Annually in strategic planning sessions or customer loyalty assessments conduct VOC research, synthesize, and summarize findings into fundamental insights of customer needs.	30%	• **AB1:** Obtain and enhance VOC for existing and potential customers.	50%
• **G2:** Within four weeks, establish milestones on progression in changing team's perspective to focus on recurring customer revenue rather than focusing exclusively on product.	40%	• **AB2:** Develop products/services roadmaps aligned with the goals of the customer while maximizing recurring revenue opportunity.	60%
• **G3:** Monthly during budget and sales review, apply financial analysis to assess growth opportunities.	20%	• **AB3:** Facilitate sessions with their team, discussing with them the ways in which they help to improve key financial metrics.	50%
• **G4:** After the company's annual plan is finalized, translate enterprise strategies into my own strategy and annual operating plan.	10%	• **AB4:** Lay out planned activities and corresponding monetary resources for the fiscal year, including recurring annual expenses and nonrecurring investments in special projects.	35%

Figure 8: Predicted Adoption Rates for Business Acumen Training

should address these concerns. Teams continue the Fist-to-Five process until they achieve consensus (a minimum of three fingers or higher) or determine that they must move on to the next adoption rate.

4. Repeat this process until all adoption rates have been agreed to.

5. Record the adoption rates on the flip chart that contains the Adoptive Behaviors.

The completed Adoption Rate Worksheet for BAT is shown in Figure 8.

To summarize, if we train 100 participants, 30 should author goals similar to Intention Goal 1. Goal 1 leads to Adoptive Behavior 1 with an Adoption Rate of 50 percent; 50 percent of 30 participants equals 15, the predicted number of employees from the 100 trained who will successfully adopt behavior 1. The goal distribution analysis for training 100 employees in BAT is shown in the following chart:

Goal/Adoptive Behavior	Distribution of Goals	# of Participants Who Author This Goal	Adoption Rate	# of Participants Predicted to Adopt Successfully
GI / ABI	30%	30	50%	15
G2 / AB2	40%	40	60%	24
G3 / AB3	20%	20	50%	10
G4 / AB4	10%	10	35%	4
Total	**100%**	**100**		**53**

Predict Adoption Value

Adoption Value is the annual result of an Adoptive Behavior being performed by one participant in monetary terms. Each result is worth something to the company. If it isn't, why include it in the course? This is where expert performers, subject matter experts, Human Resource professionals, and individuals from the Finance organization can provide input into the value. The Committee defines the expected (predicted) impact on the business, based on the assumption that course participants who have these goals and beliefs and have adopted the behaviors will produce predicted results. The Committee answers this question: *What results are realized when a participant successfully implements the Adoptive Behavior?* The *Adoptive Value Worksheet* (Figure 9) may be used to capture the Adoptive Values.

Adoptive Behaviors	Adoption Value
	What annual results are realized when a participant successfully implements the Adoptive Behavior?
• **AB1:**	
• **AB2:**	
• **AB3:**	
• **AB4:**	

Figure 9: Adoptive Value Worksheet

To predict Adoptive Value use the following steps:

1. Work one Adoptive Value at a time. Start by reviewing its associated Adoptive Behavior.

2. Use a silent brainstorming technique to generate initial member's thoughts on value—each being recorded on an individual post-it note. Post the initial value statements on the wall.

3. Use an affinity process to arrive at the salient impact items.

4. Follow with a whole-group discussion. This step is crucial in the process, and adequate time must be reserved for the conversation. At times, when the value is easily defined and straightforward, the discussion is brief. When value is a bit more difficult to define, more time is necessary. Note: The basis of these impact statements may be found in the needs analysis work that was conducted as part of the instructional design (assuming that the analysis was completed). Potential impact indicators can often be found in annual operating plans and/or strategic plans. If these plans are available, ask the Committee to review them prior to the meetings to build the impact statements. Accountants, fiscal managers, and members of the design team can assist in estimating this value by checking company records or providing their insight.

5. Use the Committee's agreed-upon decision-making process to finalize the statements. Typically, this is the consensus method, but use whatever approach the Committee prefers.

Continuing with the BAT example, the Adoptive Values were the following:

- AB1: $5,000 Adoption Value
- AB2: $10,000 Adoption Value

- AB3: $7,500 Adoption Value

- AB4: $5,000 Adoption Value

At times, Committee members can get stuck on predicting value or get mired down in impact statements that need to be raised to a higher level of value. One technique that works to get members to "move up" the impact chain is to use the *"yes and"* method. You start with an adoptive behavior and ask a question that begins with *yes and* to the statement, in order to get the next higher level of value. Follow the example to see how the method works:

Question: If salespeople perform this behavior, what would the outcome be?

Answer: They would increase their pipeline of leads.

Question: Yes and if they accomplished that, what would the result be?

Answer: It would increase their number of orders by 10 percent per month.

Question: Yes and how much value is that?

Answer: An average of $2,500 per month per sales person.

Question: Yes and if they increased their sales by $2,500 per month per person, what would that do?

Answer: The Sales Division would exceed its annual sales by 10 percent.

Question: Yes and if we exceed our sales projections by 10 percent for the year, what would that do?

Answer: Our company's Operating Profit would increase from 10.4 to 10.6 percent.

Question: Yes and what would that represent to the bottom line?

Answer: It would increase it by $500M annually.

This method allows you to draw a direct line from an Adoptive Behavior to predicted organizational and business impact.

Define the External Contribution Factor

Results that employees realize may be attributed to training, but other organizational forces could affect them also. These forces may include elements directly controlled by the company (internal forces) and those external to the company. Examples of internal forces are new product introduction, price changes, new Human Resources processes, change in strategy/annual operating plans, new leadership, mergers and acquisitions, changes in compensation plans, etc. Examples of external forces are new competition, government regulations, local/global economic conditions, etc. For example, if the Steering Committee predicts a $10,000 value from an adopted behavior, internal and external forces have contributed to that amount to some degree. This needs to be recognized and accounted for so that a more accurate prediction of training value is created. To define the External Contribution Factor, use the following guidelines:

1. This works best in teams. Divide Committee members into teams, with each team being tasked with defining the External Contribution Factor for a single Adoptive Value. Use the *External Contribution Factor Worksheet* (Figure 10).

2. List the Adoptive Behaviors and Adoption Value in the first two columns.

3. Each team then answers the question: *What forces beyond training contribute to this value?* Teams brainstorm the various forces that could affect Adoption Value, reach agreement to the salient forces, and record them on the worksheet.

4. Next, teams answer the question: *What percentage of the value do these forces contribute to the Adoption Value?*

5. Record their answers in the last column.

6. Bring the teams together and have each team present its suggestion. Facilitate the discussion, gain consensus, and finalize the External Contribution Factors. Post these on the wall for all to see.

Adoptive Behaviors	Adoption Value	Forces Contributing to Value	External Contribution Factor
		What forces beyond training contribute to this value?	*What percentage of the value do these forces contribute to the Adoption Value?*
• **AB1:**			
• **AB2:**			
• **AB3:**			
• **AB4:**			

Figure 10: External Contribution Factor Worksheet

For the BAT, External Contribution Factors (Figure 11) were as follows:

Adoptive Behaviors	Adoption Value	Forces Contributing to Value	External Contribution Factor
		What forces beyond training contribute to this value?	*What percentage of the value do these forces contribute to the Adoption Value?*
• **AB1:** Obtain and enhance VOC for existing and potential customers.	$ 5,000	• CRM system (internal) • New customer service system (external)	75%
• **AB2:** Develop products/services roadmaps aligned with the goals of the customer while maximizing recurring revenue opportunity.	$10,000	• "Omega" product release (internal) • Price increases (internal)	50%
• **AB3:** Facilitate sessions with their team, discussing with them the ways in which they help to improve key financial metrics.	$ 7,500	• Financial Services Modeling system (internal)	75%
• **AB4:** Lay out planned activities and corresponding monetary resources for the fiscal year, including recurring annual expenses and nonrecurring investments in special projects.	$ 5,000	• Strategic Planning Process (internal) • Competition for GENX product line (external) • Sales results (internal and external)	50%

Figure 11: Business Acumen Training External Contribution Factors

This is interpreted as that for Adoptive Behavior 1, 75 percent of the $5,000 value is coming from the two forces (Customer Relationship Management [CRM] system and the new customer service system). This calculates that $5,625 of the $7,000 from applying the new skills is coming from something other than training. Another way to look at it is that one participant successfully adopting behavior 1 provides an annual impact of $1,750 that is the direct result of training.

Building the Impact Matrix

The Steering Committee has accomplished a good deal to get to this point. To recap, you have the following predictive elements in place: Beliefs, Intention Goals, Adoptive Behaviors, Distribution of Goals, Adoption Rate, Adoption Value, and External Contribution Factors. These are all the elements needed to calculate annual impact per participant using the *Impact Matrix*. The Matrix uses simple formulas to calculate training's predicted impact. Let's take a look at the Business Acumen Training's Impact Matrix and work through each element (Figure 12).

A	B	C	D	E	F	G	H
Goal/ Adoptive Behavior	**Distribution of Goals**	**# of Participants Who Will Author This Goal**	**Adoption Rate**	**# of Participants Predicted to Sucessfully Adopt**	**Adoption Value**	**External Contribution Factor**	**Impact for I Year**
G1/AB1	30%	30	50%	15	$5,000	75%	$56,250
G2/AB2	40%	40	60%	24	$10,000	50%	$120,000
G3/AB3	20%	20	50%	10	$7,500	75%	$56,250
G4/AB4	10%	10	35%	4	$5,000	50%	$10,000
	100%	**100**		**53**			

No. of Participants per Year   100   **Impact of I year**   **$242,500**

Figure 12: Impact Matrix for Business Acumen Training

Impact Matrix Element	**Description**
No. of Participants per Year	Number of participants that are to be trained on an annual basis.
Column A: Goal/Adoptive Behavior	Intention Goals and the associated Adoptive Behaviors for the course. List one goal/behavior per row.
Column B: Distribution of Goals	Percentage of participants who author the goal and attempt to adopt the behavior. Note: percentage need to sum to 100 percent.
Column C: No. of Participants to Author This Goal	*Calculated Value:* no. of participants who are expected to author this Intention Goal and therefore attempt to transfer the Adoptive Behavior. The formula is *(Number of Participants) x (Goal Distribution Percentage)* or *(Number of Participants) x (Column B)*
Column D: Adoption Rate	Percentage of participants predicted to adopt the behavior successfully.
Column E: No. of Participants Predicted to Adopt Successfully	*Calculated Value:* no. of participants who successfully adopt the behavior. The formula is *(No. of Participants who Author This Goal) x (Adoption Rate)* or *(Column C) x (Column D)*

(Continued...)

Impact Matrix Element	**Description**
Column F: Adoption Value	Annual result of an Adoptive Behavior being performed by one participant in monetary terms.
Column G: External Contribution Factor	Percentage that other influences beyond training contribute to results.
Column H: Impact for I Year	*Calculated Value:* predicted impact participants will deliver on an annual basis. The formula is

(No. of Participants Predicted to Adopt Successfully) x (Adoption Value) x (External Contribution Factor)

or

(Column E) x (Column F) x (Column G)

Perform this for all Intention Goals and Adoptive Behaviors. The predicted **Impact for one year** for training 100 employees in Business Acumen is $242,500.

Produce the Impact Matrix and present it to the Steering Committee for review and a "sanity check." Ask the Committee these questions: *Do the results look reasonable? What flaws do we have in the Matrix that would cause us to have an inaccurate prediction? Can you support this?* If items need changed, modify as necessary and recreate the Matrix. Once the Committee is satisfied, post the Impact Matrix on the wall.

Predict Training's Return on Investment

Is $242,500 attractive to key decision makers? How much will it cost to produce this impact? What is the return for this investment? Should we invest our scarce resources on training, or would the funds be better spent somewhere else? These are all good questions that can be answered by calculating training's Return on Investment (ROI). ROI is a measure of the productivity of a firm's assets (in this case, money) and is a performance measure used to evaluate the efficiency of an investment or to compare the efficiency of a number of different investments. To calculate ROI, the benefit (return) of an investment is divided by the cost of the investment; the result is expressed as a percentage or a ratio. For training's ROI, the predicted impact (benefit) is divided by the cost of the training. The training return on investment formula is as follows:

$$\text{Training ROI} = \frac{\text{Predicted Impact}}{\text{Cost of Training}}$$

Return on investment is a popular metric because of its versatility and simplicity. As with any investment analysis, if training does not have a positive ROI or if there are other opportunities with a higher ROI, training should not be undertaken.

You already have the *Predicted Impact* from the Impact Matrix that you created. Because impact is an *annual* value, you need annual training costs. To calculate annual training costs, you estimate the expenses. Typical expenses are the following:

- **Design**: One-time cost for instructional design. If this is a redesign, enter the cost for the redesign effort.

- **Development**: One-time cost for creating the training materials. If this is a redesign, enter the cost for redevelopment.

- **Delivery**: Annual cost to deliver training. For classroom delivery, items usually included in this cost include the following:
  - Instructor(s) fees
  - License fees
  - Training room fees
  - Material purchase/reproduction costs
  - Equipment costs (depending on the course). Note: These may be depreciated over the life span of the course.
  - Travel fees: instructor and/or participants
  - Food

  Note: some companies calculate participant labor cost while in training and lost opportunity costs.

- **Evaluation**: Cost for Intention, Adoption, and Impact evaluation work that is incurred annually for the life of the course.

- **Total cost:** Calculated Value: total annual cost for training. The formula is

  Total Cost = (Design) + (Development) + (Delivery) + (Evaluation)

- **Number of participants per year:** Number of participants to be trained per year

- **Cost per participant:** Calculated Value: annual cost to train one participant. The formula is: Cost per Participant = (Total Cost) / (Number of participants per year)

The Steering Committee needs to agree to the cost projections. Once that is complete, you now can calculate the ROI for training. Figure 13 shows the ROI for BAT.

	Year 1 (100 participants)		Year 2 (100 participants)		Year 3 (100 participants)	
	Cost	Impact	Cost	Impact	Cost	Impact
Year 1	$250,000	$242,500				
Year 2	$0	$242,500	$205,000	$242,500		
Year 3	$0	$242,500	$0	$242,500	$205,000	$242,500
Total	**$250,000**	**$727,500**	**$205,000**	**$485,000**	**$205,000**	**$242,500**

	ROI	291%	ROI	237%	ROI	118%

Lifetime Cost	$660,000
Lifetime Impact	$1,455,000
Value of Training for 3 Years	$795,000
ROI for 3 Years	220%

Figure 13: ROI for Business Acumen Training

Business Acumen Training has a projected life span of three years, with 100 employees being trained annually. Looking at the year-1 cohort (the group of employees trained in that year), it costs $250,000 in year 1 to train them (design + development + delivery + evaluation). The annual predicted impact is $242,500, which sums to three years of a cumulative impact of $727,500. Employees trained in year 2 have no costs or impact in year 1 of BAT's life span, but they do have cost in year 2 ($205,000) and two years' worth of impact ($485,000). Employees trained in year 3 have no costs or impact in years 1 and 2, but they do have one year of cost ($205,000) and impact $242,500). Each year has an ROI calculated. Completing the ROI analysis for three years, BAT will cost $660,000 train 300 employees. The predicted impact from the 300 employees is $1,455,000, giving us a value of training of $795,000 result-ing in three-year ROI of 220 percent.

Companies usually have defined hurdles (minimum ROI) that investments need to achieve before key decision makers approve the investment. Check with your Finance department and use whatever values it has set.

Payback Period

One way a Steering Committee can look at the ROI to determine whether it is attractive is via the *Payback Period*. This is investment's payback period in years, equal to the net investment amount divided by the average annual cash flow from the investment. **What does it mean?** How long will it take to get my money back? The **strengths** of using Payback Period are that it's easy to compute, easy to understand, and provides some indication of risk by separating long-term projects from short-term projects. The **weakness** is that it doesn't measure profitability, account for the time value of money,[4] and ignores financial performance after the breakeven period. Payback period is the most widely used measure for evaluating potential investments. Its use increases in tough economic times, when CEOs are apt to say things like, "We won't even consider a project that has more than a 24-month payback."

The data show that BAT pays for itself just after one year. The Steering Committee reviews the data and answers questions such as these: *When will training payback its investment? Is this within company guidelines? Is the ROI attractive? How does training's ROI compare with other investments?* Note: your company may choose to analyze investments by means of Net Present Value. If this is the case, enlist the aid of the Finance department to aid with this calculation and analysis.

After building these data, the Steering Committee decides whether to move forward with the training or not.

Step 4: Validate the Matrix

The Steering Committee has done some outstanding work, but it is in draft form. It is a best practice to validate the Matrix with other parties to ensure that the predictions are as accurate as they can possibly be. The steps in a validation process are the following:

1. Seek suggestions from Committee members on who should be included in the validation process. Possible validation parties are the following:
   - For existing training, past participants. For new training, future participants.
   - Expert performers
   - Stakeholders for the training: a person or a group who has a vested interest in the training and who may be affected by it. This is usually executives who send employees to training.
   - Finance specialists
   - External consultants
   - Course designers, developers, and instructors (if they were not represented when the Steering Committee created the Impact Matrix)
2. Establish a validation protocol, which constitutes the methods by which you seek feedback on the Matrix. A variety of methods may be used, such as surveys, focus groups, and one-on-one interviews.
3. Collect feedback using defined protocol. Collect enough data so that you can adequately present your finding to the Committee.

Step 5: Finalize the Matrix

Summarize findings and convene a Steering Committee meeting to share the results. When summarizing findings, ask yourself this question: *Where do we have strong agreement with the Matrix? Where do we have strong disagreement? What changes, if any, would I recommend to the Committee based on my analysis?* The Committee is relying on you to advise them on changes.

Present the findings and facilitate a discussion. Usually, the members can agree to the changes, and the Matrix is finalized. Sometimes certain elements of the Matrix need to be reworked. If they are minor and you have the time, facilitate the meeting and agree to the changes. If the changes are more substantial, form a sub-team to work on them and report back to the Committee. The output is an Impact Matrix that can be presented to key decision makers.

Step 6: Present the Impact Matrix to Key Decision Makers for Approval

It is time to present the Impact Matrix to key decision makers for approval to move forward with the training or not. Hopefully, they will make the decision as they do with other investments: based on the attractiveness of the return to the business. The first step of decision making is for key decision makers to recognize and define the problem or opportunity—in our case, the need for training. Instead of leading with a three-day sales training course, lead with the business problem that training could help correct. The second part of decision-making process is to identify and analyze alternative courses of action (to train or not to train) and estimate their effects on the problem or opportunity or other parts of the business. If I train, what will I not be able to do? Showing training's ROI, Simple Payback, or Net Present Value calculations allows decision makers to judge the training investment on similar grounds with other investments. The third step in decision making is for the executives to choose a preferred course of action using the analysis tools that the Committee has presented.

Here are some tips as you prepare for the presentation:

1. Have the Steering Committee make the presentations. It is their Impact Matrix, and they should be the ones providing the information.

2. Keep it short and simple—two to three slides at most. The most important slide is the Impact Matrix. It is written in business language and clearly delineates what the company will be receiving for its investment. Spend most of your time here.

3. *Why are you delivering this presentation?* Answer: to inform them of the business issue(s) that training could solve and the forecast return

on the investment. *What do the executives think now, and what do you want them to think?* Answer: Most likely they now think of training as an expense and a set of classes. You want them to think that training solves business problems and returns value to the company.

Summary

Using a series of tools and techniques, you have predicted training's value. The impact you have calculated is aligned with the course design and provides a best estimate of return. Armed with this data, key decision makers now make an informed decision: if they train, they know what return can be expected. This is the **predictive** component of PE. The remaining chapters in this book are devoted to the **evaluation** elements of PE.

Chapter 3

Intention Evaluation

An Intention Evaluation (IE) addresses the following question: *Are participant goals and beliefs upon course completion aligned with desired goals?* The steps to conduct a successful IE are the following:

Step 1: Establish the Success Gate for Intention Goals

Step 2: Establish the Success Gate for Beliefs

Step 3: Capture Goals and Beliefs

Step 4: Compare Goals against Standard

Step 5: Calculate Intention Goals and Beliefs Scores

Step 6: Analyze and React

Step 7: Create Intention Dashboard

Step 1: Establish the Success Gate for Intention Goals

An Intention Goals Success Gate is the percentage of goals written by participants that are judged as matching the goals created when you predicted training's values (see Chapter 2). For example, if an Intention Goals Success Gate is set at 90 percent and fifty goals are authored by participants, the 90 percent success gate requires that forty-five of those goals be judged as acceptable (as matching the predicted Intention Goals).

Establishing an Intention Goals Success Gate is not difficult. Sometimes, you, the evaluator, nominate a percentage, based on experience with the type of training being delivered. In other cases, it is set by the Steering Committee. Usually the Success Gate is set high, such as 90 percent. Steering Committee members ask, "Why is it so high?" The rationale is that the right goals lead to an increased adoption level, and we want to maximize training's adoption, thus resulting in maximum value gained. Another way to think about it is to consider training to be a factory producing highly skilled workers. What defect rate does the company expect from its real factories? The answer is "as close to zero as possible." We know that we are dealing with people and not widgets, so zero defects are unreasonable, but the concept is the same.

You want as many participants planning to do the right thing as possible. Keeping that in mind, the most common Intention Goal Success Gate is 90 percent.

Consider the size of each class when setting the Success Gate. For example, 90 percent for a class size of twenty participants with two goals each means that only four goals can be rejected.

Step 2: Establish the Success Gate for Beliefs

PE suggests that training should not only provide knowledge and skill but instill the proper belief(s). Beliefs are defined as "the idea that the participants and/or their company will benefit from using the new knowledge and skills." We can set belief expectations and measure them if training has instilled those beliefs. In other words, do our participants believe what we want them to believe? Beliefs for a course were documented in the Predict Training's Value tasks (Chapter 2).

Once you predict the belief statements, you can measure if the course is generating the proper beliefs using a semantic differential. A semantic differential is a type of a rating scale designed to measure the connotative meaning of objects, events, and concepts. The connotations are used to derive the attitude toward the given object, event, or concept. PE uses a seven-point differential (ratings 1 through 7), where 1 represents a *Meaningless* belief and 7 represents a *Meaningful* belief.

Set the Success Gate for Beliefs (predict what the results should be). This is usually done by the Steering Committee. One technique is to use the "Top Box score" approach used with customer satisfaction analyses. Top Box score includes only "high belief" participants, for example, a Beliefs Success Gate could be that *90 percent of our participants choose a rating 6 or 7*, with the values of 6 or 7 being classified as Top Box. Another Success Gate is where the mean values of the Beliefs ratings are used. An example of a Success Gate using mean values is this: *the mean value of the Beliefs results will be 6.3 or greater on a 7-point semantic differential scale.*

Step 3: Capture Goals and Beliefs

During and at the close of training, participants author their goals and rate their beliefs. These are written during a goal-planning (sometimes called action-planning) section in the course. In general, participants can realistically accomplish two or three goals after a training program. If they write more, they often accomplish relatively little, which results in low or no adoption.

The first task is to create the goal-planning sheet to collect Intention Goals and Beliefs.

Goal Planning Guidelines

Purpose of goal planning: the goal sheet (or action plan) is a set of clearly written statements describing in measurable terms the specific actions the participant intends to apply on-the-job as a result of training. In preparing this, the participant is drawing up a personal transfer plan, thinking about how, where, and when to match the new skills to concrete situations on-the-job before leaving training. Participants may also be asked to think through potential obstacles to transfer and how to overcome those.[1]

This goal-setting strategy enhances the likelihood of adoption. Once back at work and confronted with e-mails, phone calls, meetings, and problems, the participant's intention to adopt is negatively impacted—few participants take time in the two or three days after training to think about how they will use what they have just learned and practiced.

I have found a significant increase in training transfer (adoption) when participants set goals before returning to work. The majority attempt to implement at least one item. I also found that when participants show goal sheets to their supervisors, the likelihood of adoption is significantly increased. However, supervisors should include some form of accountability with their direct reports when the participants return from training.

Components of goal planning sheets are the following:

1. Clear instructions about what is required (e.g., how many items, if one item must reflect a specific content section, if items must conform to a format)

2. Criteria for judging items as acceptable

3. Worked example on the goal-planning sheet so that participants can use it as a guide. The example should reflect the course content. It should be written at a high level of specificity because participants rarely write beyond the level of detail of the example.

4. Space to write their goals

Incorporating Goal Planning into a Course

Provide the goal-planning sheet in the participant materials and provide notes for the instructor, explaining the purpose of the activity, how to introduce it, how much time to allocate, and criteria for acceptable action items. Allocate time at the end of the program to write goals. As a rule of thumb, participants need fifteen to thirty minutes to write two goals. In some cases, more time is required than this. Participants who are technical workers rather than knowledge workers may take longer. They may experience difficulty articulating on paper what they want to write and need the instructor to help them.

What constitutes a good goal? A correctly written goal meets the three criteria of the SOS + D (Specific, Observable, Significant, and Directly related) model:

- **Specific:** The goal is free of ambiguity, and it is clear what the participant will be doing.

- **Observable:** Others will be able to see the participant doing this.

- **Significant:** The implementation of the goal will make a real difference to the participant, his or her team, and the company.

Furthermore, and the goals must be

- **Directly related:** The goal flows out of the course content.

The typical Intention Goal elements on a goal planning form are the following:

- **Which sections of the training does this goal relate to (choose all that apply)?** List the training modules for the participant to choose from. This section is used to capture goal distribution data (with what modules of the course have participants aligned their goal?).

- **I will (describe what you plan to do).** This is the action that the participant plans to undertake. Instruct participants to include two components of the SOS + D goal model in this part of their goal: *Situation* and *Observable* action.

- **The outcome I expect from doing this is.** This is the desired result(s) that participants hope to realize when they implement their action. This is the *Significant* element of the SOS + D goal model.

If you plan to have participants author more than a single goal, repeat the preceding statements for each goal. You can print goal-planning worksheets on two-part carbonless paper, with the top copy going to the evaluation team for processing and the participant retaining the bottom portion (carbon copy). In some courses, the goal-planning worksheet can be created in a Web-based format. Participants enter their final goals on their laptops. In this situation, the paper form is used to draft their goals before entering them electronically. See Figure 14 for the BAT goal planning sheet.

Please enter your *Business Acumen Training* post-program goal. The goal sheet that you send to V.A.L.E. Consulting will remain confidential. Only evaluators will see them.

General Information

First name: _____   Last name: _____

My e-mail: _____   Training location (city, state): _____

Date training started: ____ / ____ / ____   Instructor's name: _____

Instructions: List the actions you will take as soon as you leave this training, putting what you have learned into practice. Your goals should be **directly related** to course content, should reflect the skills taught in class, and should be …

Specific to your role and challenges, starting tomorrow

Observable, allowing others to see you doing these things

Significant, making a real difference to you, your team, or the company

My Goal

Which sections of the training does this goal relate to (choose all that apply)?

☐ Strategy into Action   ☐ Financial Analysis and Interpretation

☐ Assessing Business Opportunities   ☐ In Pursuit of Legendary Customer Experiences

☐ Innovation and Creativity as Drivers of Strategic Change

I will … (as specifically as possible, describe what you will do)

The outcome I expect from doing this is …

How meaningful are the following statements to you?

	Meaningless						Meaningful
Business leaders must operate with a customer-centric focus ············	1	2	3	4	5	6	7
Customer intimacy is a transformative strategy that results in improved sales, service, and overall satisfaction ············	1	2	3	4	5	6	7
Successful execution of strategy is a function of thinking, planning, action, and learning ············	1	2	3	4	5	6	7
Use of appropriate metrics drive accountability and results ············	1	2	3	4	5	6	7
Innovation is a key to sustainable and profitable growth ············	1	2	3	4	5	6	7

Figure 14: BAT Goal Planning Sheet

Make Your Goal Planning Successful

- Introduce goal planning at the beginning of training, and stress the importance to the participants that they have the responsibility for planning and executing their new skills on-the-job.

- If you have a multi-day program, you may want the participants to journal their goal ideas and reflect on what they have learned and will possibly use during the goal-planning session.

- Teach goal construction (the SOS + D model). Most participants are not good at writing goals and need clear instructions.

- Provide examples of goals that do and do not meet the SOS + D model.

- Have a peer review and give feedback on goals.

- Instructors review and asking probing questions to ensure that the goal reflects what the participant can and wants to do.

- Keep the goal form simple, and allow adequate time for participants to reflect, compose, get feedback, and finalize their intentions.

Step 4: Compare Goals against Standard

After participants have left training, the evaluator judges each goal and compares it to the predicted goals from the Impact Matrix's Intentions Goal. If possible, use two evaluators to independently judge the goals and then jointly decide on those that are acceptable. Two evaluators provide a higher level of reliability in judging goals. The following checklist is used in judging goals. Goals from participants never exactly match predicted goals. Use your best judgment, be consistent, and use the SOS + D model as your guide.

Judging Intention Goals

Criteria	√
Specific	Goal is free of ambiguity and specifies exactly what the participant will be doing.
Observable	Actions will be noticed, visible, or discernible when the participant is doing them.
Significant	Results will make a difference (impact) and provide value to the individual, team, or the company.
Directly Related	Goal is aligned to course content

An acceptable goal is one that meets all four criteria. The process for this step is the following:

1. Collect goal-planning sheets (hardcopy or electronically) from participants.

2. Enter goals into an analysis spreadsheet.

3. Read each goal.

4. Goals that have the SOS + D components *and* for which what is written are similar to an Intention Goal on the Impact Matrix are judged as acceptable. Goals that are missing an SOS + D component *or* for which what is written does not align with an Intention Goal on the Impact Matrix are judged as unacceptable.

Intention data are organized into a data structure (spreadsheet or database) with one record per participant. A typical data structure is as follows:

Learner Demographic Data
- Course name
- First name
- Last name
- Role
- E-mail
- Training start date
- Training location
- Instructor

Goal Data
- Course module
- I will . . .
- The outcome I expect is . . .
- *Acceptable Y/N*
- *Evaluator comments*

Belief Data
- Belief Rating

Data elements in the preceding normal text are captured and entered into the database from the goal-planning form. Italic texts are data entered by the evaluator.

Step 5: Calculate Intention Goals and Beliefs Scores

Using a spreadsheet, apply the following formula to determine the Intention Goals and Beliefs Scores:

$$\text{Intention Score} = \frac{\text{Acceptable Goals}}{\text{Total Goals}}$$

$$\text{Beliefs Score} = \frac{\text{\# of Beliefs Rated Top Box}}{\text{Total Belief Ratings}}$$

With respect to Intention Evaluation, a single delivery of a course is deemed successful when (1) the Intention Score equals or exceeds the Intention Goals Success Gate *and* (2) the Beliefs Score equals or exceeds the Beliefs Success Gate. For classroom deliveries, courses have a start and end date that easily define the single delivery. For online training, you set the start and end dates for Intention Evaluation's single delivery (e.g., all course completions in the second quarter).

Step 6: Analyze and React

Compare the Intention Goals Score against the Intentions Success Gate. If it is greater, the course is working as planned, and no corrective action is needed. If it is lower, the evaluator must investigate further to determine why (root cause) and what correction action to recommend.

Steps to determine root cause include the following:

1. Review the goals judged as unacceptable. Is there a pattern as to why they did not meet the standard? Are they missing the situation from the SOS + D model? Are the observable components of the goals vague or nearly impossible to observe? Does the significance section of the goals fail to state the desired impact? If these are the case, solutions that may correct this issue are as follows:

   a. Train instructors, facilitators, or coaches to ensure that goals are structured properly.

   b. Provide examples in class for participants to model their goals on.

   c. Consider adding more time during the course for goal development, receiving feedback, and finalizing goals if time in the agenda allows.

2. Some goals may meet the SOS + D format but have nothing to do with course content. In other words, the goal may add value for the individual but does not reflect any skill or knowledge from the course. For example, this goal came from a participant who attended a First-Time Managers course: *"When I hold meetings with my staff, I will not wear my headband with the words DA BOSS on it."* It was a laudable goal and, most likely, right for this individual, except that the course had no "dress for success" content. Therefore, the goal was not aligned with an Intentions Goal on the Impact Matrix and

was judged unacceptable. The solution is to ensure that instructors or coaches clarify with participants that they must write goals that are aligned with the training.

3. Analysis of unacceptable goals may suggest that the course does not teach what is necessary for participants to author goals that meet predefined standards. In this case, a review and possible changes to the course content may be warranted.

4. Sometimes people other than the intended audience attend training and, because of the nature of their role and/or experience, they write unacceptable goals. A review/modification to the enrollment procedure may be warranted.

5. Finally, instructors may be teaching their own content and may not be following the course as designed. In this case, an observation of the instructor, along with a performance improvement plan, may be helpful.

Step 7: Create Intention Dashboard

There are times where we as evaluators, trainers, and Human Resources professionals need to convey training evaluation findings. Often we spend hours authoring a detailed report, making sure every word is just so. In fact, the only people who read these reports are us. Our business partners don't have the time or the desire to read an eighteen-page report with an appendix and glossary of terms.

In PE, we share our findings using the dashboard concept. The dashboard is a report to senior management that provides an at-a-glance perspective on the current status of a course in the context of predetermined metrics for that program (Intention, Adoption, or Impact). Good dashboards are simple, short, and do not require you to interpret them.

Dashboard reports are used to allow managers and executives to examine and assess training success. They facilitate discussion by highlighting metric status points, encouraging management by exception, when deviations from the norm become the focal points of discussion.

As the name implies, the dashboard report often takes on the look and feel of an instrument panel in a car or plane. It is a set of graphic representations of the evaluation information that is important to management. For an Intention Dashboard, I suggest using a three-page PowerPoint deck that contains the following:

- Page 1: the charts and graphs that provide, at a glance, the evaluation results. This is the "instrument panel" of the dashboard. Also included are evaluator comments, which allow the evaluator to provide interpretation of the data and any other circumstances, such as organizational factors, that have influenced the result.

- Page 2: example goals from participants. Whereas the first page is the instrument panel of the dashboard, this section is the heart and soul of the evaluation data, describing what employees plan to do with their new skills and knowledge.

- Page 3: examples of unacceptable goals and the reasons why they were judged so.

Perhaps the greatest danger associated with dashboard reports is that management may believe that they understand the intricacies of the training by virtue of this limited amount of information. They sometimes must be reminded that reading a dashboard report makes one no more aware of the details of training than reading the indicators on a car's dashboard makes one a mechanic. It's a quick, effective overview of critical metrics. Dashboards are created based on volume of classes (monthly, quarterly, or whenever a program occurs). Frequency of reporting is based on volume and the needs of the Steering Committee.

The dashboard tells the reader (most likely the Steering Committee) how the program is working with respect to Intentions.

Intention Dashboard, Page 1 (Figure 15)

The first page of an Intention Dashboard typically has five sections.

Section 1: Title. "Intention Evaluation: Course Title" plus the time period, such as month and year.

Section 2: Intention Success Gate. The Intentions Success Gate shows, at a glance, what classes (sessions) have met the Intention Goals, Beliefs, and overall Intention Success Gates. Data are sorted by month with each class (session), showing its Goal Score, Belief Score, and whether or not the class meets its Intention expectation. For this example, the Intention Goals and Belief Score have a Success Gate of 90 percent. When an Intention Goals or Belief Score falls below the Success Gate, the cell is shaded gray. If either the Intention Goals or Belief Score is below the Success Gate, the class does not meet the Intention Success Gate, and the cell is shaded gray and an "N" is placed in that cell. At the bottom of the table, the percentage of classes for the month that have met the Intention Success Gate are shown.

Intention Dashboard Page 1

	Jan			Feb			Mar		
	Goal Score	Belief Score	Succ. Gate of 90%?	Goal Score	Belief Score	Succ. Gate of 90%?	Goal Score	Belief Score	Succ. Gate of 90%?
Class 1	91%	94%	Y	88%	92%	N	98%	85%	N
Class 2	98%	90%	Y	81%	99%	N	100%	99%	Y
Class 3	89%	100%	N	98%	92%	Y	98%	92%	Y
Class 4	95%	99%	Y	80%	97%	N	100%	93%	Y
Class 5	85%	93%	N	93%	93%	N	90%	85%	Y
Class 6	88%	96%	N	81%	94%	N	90%	85%	Y
Class 7	81%	88%	N	94%	99%	Y	100%	100%	Y
Class 8	84%	97%	N	84%	85%	N	92%	96%	Y
Class 9	69%	94%	N	87%	98%	N	93%	89%	Y
Class 10	85%	97%	N	80%	91%	N	96%	81%	Y
% classes succ.			30%			20%			90%

Evaluator Comments for March

- 267 students authored 463 goals and rated 5 beliefs.
- The quality of goal statements is markedly improved on previous months. Several classes had 100% acceptable goals. Only 1 class fell below the success gate.
- The goals around Strategy into Action are difficult to write in observable terms, but there are a number of good ones in the March goals. Instructors have done a good job helping participants articulate their goals in behavioral language.

Belief Score: % rating 6 or 7 (1 = meaningless, 7 = meaningful)	
93%	Business leaders must operate with a customer-centric focus.
79%	Customer intimacy is a transformative strategy that results in improved sales, service, and overall satisfaction.
95%	Successful execution of strategy is a function of thinking, planning, action, and learning.
90%	Use of appropriate metrics drives accountability and results.
91%	Innovation is a key to sustainable and profitable growth.

Goal Distribution

Legend:
- Innovation and Creativity as Drivers of Strategic Change
- In Pursuit of Legendary Customer Experiences
- Assessing Business Opportunities
- Financial Analysis & Interpretation
- Strategy into Action

	Jan	Fab	Mar
Innovation and Creativity as Drivers of Strategic Change	10%	14%	11%
In Pursuit of Legendary Customer Experiences	29%	22%	26%
Assessing Business Opportunities	25%	25%	24%
Financial Analysis & Interpretation	24%	25%	24%
Strategy into Action	12%	14%	15%

Figure 15: Intention Dashboard, Page 1

Figure 15 is actual data from a PE. As you can see by examining the data, the course was not meeting its Intention Success Gates for January and February. These two months were the first time that instructors were teaching a redesigned version of the course. An analysis revealed two reasons for the low results: (1) two modules in the course were not working as designed and (2) instructors were allowing poorly written goals. The course was redesigned, additional examples of Intention Goals were developed, and a meeting with the instructors was held at the end of February to correct the goal-writing activities. March results were stellar—in fact, Intention Scores for the rest of year were outstanding.

Section 3: Goal Distribution Chart. The Goal Distribution Chart shows the distribution of goals authored by participants. In this case, for BAT, the five course modules are graphed. This dashboard chart tells the reader the dispersion of goals among participants. These actual results can be compared to predicted results in the Impact Matrix.

Section 4: Belief Results Table. This table shows the percentage of participants whose belief responses were as predicted. In this case, a predicted value is a rating of 6 or 7 on the goal sheet (or Top Box). The Beliefs Success Gate of 90 percent was clearly met for all but one of the beliefs.

Section 5: Evaluator Comments. This section allows you, the evaluator, to provide whatever commentary you wish on the Intention results.

Intention Dashboard, Page 2 (Figure 16)

The second page provides examples of exemplary goals. This shows how participants have taken the content and powerfully generalized it to their specific work role.

Intention Dashboard, Page 3 (Figure 17)

The final page depicts goals that were judged unacceptable and the reasons why.

Intention Evaluation and Continuous Improvement

Training programs provide knowledge, skills, and changed beliefs. Building on this, participants develop short-term goals that are adopted and utilized on-the-job. These in turn establish the potential for delivering long-lasting business impact. If participants believe that using new skills and tools benefits them, their team, and the business, their adoption rate increases.

Intention Dashboard Page 2

Selected Exemplary Goals from Participants—March

I will find out what measures of performance are being used to monitor the financial effectiveness of my team so that I can better understand how my job links to these measures and how my efforts ultimately make an impact on the company's financial targets. My expected results is that my team will achieve a 10% profit margin in 18 months.	Find my own company's P-E ratio, market-to-book ratio, and total shareholder return so that I can lead my team to increase the value we create for shareholders with revenue growth of 15% in 3 years; and so that my team understands how we contribute to and affect total shareholder return.	Review the types of assets used by my operation, and • Evaluate which assets are more important in terms of operations and monetary value • Identify which assets I have responsibility for purchasing or utilizing so that I understand how our investments in assets of different types have different challenges. If my organization has a large percentage of current assets, we will manage those assets to increase total asset turnover to 2.0.
Document the kinds of accrued expenses in our operations that do not always match up with the actual cash payments. I will then assess the timeliness of our reporting mechanism (i.e., do we in fact report our accrued expenses according to our financial guidelines?) so that I will have a true picture of our balance sheet and income statements and so that I can be sure which items are particularly important to accrue in a timely manner relative to the overall effort to monitor and control spending.	Identify the gross profit margin, E:R ratio, and operating profit margins of the company and those of our competitors. Understand any trends or observations regarding the improvement or deterioration of the above measures over the last few years. Conduct an analysis of our product mix and make a recommendation as to how we could change it to increase gross profit. Conduct a 5-year horizontal analysis on my company so that I will understand our company's initiatives to improve all of our different profit margins by 3%–5%.	In the next few weeks I will evaluate the product mix of my division and identify the higher gross profit margin products and the proportion that they make up in our total product portfolio so that we sell as many of the higher gross profit margin products as possible, therefore increasing gross profit margin by 28%.

Figure 16: Intention Dashboard, Page 2

Intention Dashboard Page 3	
Goals judged as unacceptable—March	
Goal submitted	**Reason evaluators judged goal as unacceptable**
I will help others identify financial risk and how to do things in a more efficient manner. The outcome I expect is enable them to feel like they can and should help others do the same.	How will they help others identify financial risks? Also "help others" is vague.
I will use my statement of cash flows to more effective way with my work group and other groups. The outcome I expect is better cash.	The "I will" statement is not understandable. Outcome statement is not measurable.
I will use my business acumen skills to educate and mentor my group giving them a partnership toward financial stability. The outcome I expect is higher profits.	"Business acumen skills" is a nebulous term. What skills will they be using exactly? Action is very vague ... what will they be doing, and what will the outcomes be?

Figure 17: Intention Dashboard, Page 3

PE suggests a number of ways in which evaluative data can be used for continuous improvement of the course and enhanced post-program adoption. Here are some of the procedures to utilize if Intention Scores fall below the success gate.

Area of concern	Potential corrective actions
Participant-authored goals are weak.	• Analyze training content and application exercises. Do they teach and reinforce the proper goals as defined in the course design? • Provide participants with examples of acceptable goals. Note of caution: some evaluators try to overcome this issue by providing participants with a list of acceptable goals and having them choose from the list. It is critical that participants write their own goals, applicable to their specific work situation, even if they are provided with some examples to review.

	• The goal-writing experience and expertise of participants is weak—most likely, they do not write goals as a part of their job. Therefore, they may need help with goal construction. Set aside time in the course to teach them the SOS + D goal format. • Hang posters of acceptable goals on the classroom walls. Ask instructors to review and provide feedback. • Implement a peer review opportunity where participants share goals with each other and provide feedback. • Check that adequate time is provided to author goals. The minimum time is at least fifteen to thirty minutes. • Ensure that instructors understand the criteria for acceptable goals. Consider adding this to the train-the-trainer process and instructor guides.
Distribution of goals is skewed (too many goals relate to one module, or too few goals relate to a critical module).	• Examine the course design. Does the course spend the appropriate amount of time on each subject area? If not, consider modifying to meet desired percentage. • Investigate participant profiles. Is training being delivered to the intended target audience? If not, consider modifying enrollment process. • In an instructor-led program, are instructors teaching all sections of the course? Are they emphasizing certain sections more than others? Considering auditing the program to ensure that the course is being taught as designed. • In an E-Learning program, check if participants are bypassing sections of the course or simply "clicking through." Consider holding a focus group of participants to better understand their path through the course.
Belief statements are weak or unfocused.	• Review program design and materials to ensure that they support the belief patterns required for impact. Modify as needed.

Using PE to Improve Instructor Performance

Intention evaluation data can be a powerful instructor performance tool. For example, a two-day leadership course delivered to over 2,000 leaders in a ten-month period by an external consulting company was assessed against a success gate of 90 percent. Because of the magnitude of the effort, twenty instructors were assigned to teach the course.

During the first few months of delivery, a majority of the classes failed to meet the Intention Goals Success Gate of 90 percent. Analysis of Intention data revealed that most of the unacceptable goals were coming from classes taught by the same instructors.

A meeting was held with the instructors to educate them on goal construction and on how to work with participants to write good goals. As a result, during the following month and all months thereafter, the data were stellar. This is an excellent example of the power of PE to drive continuous improvement.

Summary

Intention Evaluation is a leading indicator of post-program adoption and subsequent business impact. It addresses the following question: *Are participant goals and beliefs upon course completion aligned with desired goals?* Intentional participants (right goals with the proper beliefs) lead to successful transfer to the workplace. Measuring Intentions against predicted results allows companies to improve training continuously so that it ensures that business and organizational results are maximized.

Chapter 4

Adoption Evaluation

An **Adoption Evaluation** addresses the following question: *How much of the training has been implemented on the job and successfully integrated into the participant's work behavior?*

An Adoption Evaluation measures participant goal completion rate against the defined Adoption Rate created when you predicted training's value (Chapter 2). Data are collected on the success that participants have had in transferring their goals to the workplace, results are analyzed and compared to the Adoption Rate, and an Adoption Dashboard is produced to report findings. If needed, corrective actions are put in place to improve adoption. The steps to conduct a successful Adoption Evaluation are as follows:

Step 1: Review the Adoption Rate Success Gate and Decide When to Collect Data

Step 2: Develop Adoption Survey

Step 3: Collect Adoption Data

Step 4: Create Adoption Dashboard

Step 5: Analyze and React

Step 1: Review the Adoption Rate Success Gate and Decide When to Collect Data

The Adoption Rate Success Gate is the percentage of participants who have successfully implemented their training goals; it is a measure of transference from the course to the workplace. The Adoption Rate for each behavior (Success Gate) was defined in the Predict Training's Value phase and is an element in the *Impact Matrix* (Chapter 2). It is the percentage of participants that we want to perform the work (Adoptive Behaviors) and the prediction of successful transfer from training to the workplace. This value becomes the metric used to evaluate the program.

Two factors need to be considered when determining when adoption has occurred. First, what is an appropriate adoption rate for a group of participants? It is unrealistic to assume that 100 percent of participants will successfully adopt the new skills. Therefore, what adoption rate is reasonable for the skill within a given company and its culture? Reference the course's Impact Matrix. Second, the length of time that participants have had to practice and integrate the new skill. This time varies by opportunity to practice and by the number of times to practice. For example, if the participant's goal was to utilize a new greeting when answering a customer service telephone call, he or she likely had dozens of times to practice the very next day. An evaluator could assume that, after a few days, he or she will adopt, or never will adopt, the behavior; therefore the data could be collected rather quickly. If the new skill is to conduct an analysis of current market trends, the time to do the work could be lengthy, and the number of times required to practice would need to be factored in.

So, depending on the skills and opportunity to practice, you determine how long after training to collect adoption data. This is a balancing act between collecting it too early (participants do not have enough opportunity to transfer) or too late (other factors have entered into the picture that may affect the results). If you are having difficulty determining when to collect, consider using two to three months after training as your guideline.

Review the Adoptive Behaviors and their associated Adoption Rates (the Success Gates) found in the Impact Matrix. Once you thoroughly understand the Adoption Rate Success Gates, you can proceed to *Step 2: Develop Adoption Survey*.

Step 2: Develop Adoption Survey

After reviewing the predicted Adoption Rate and deciding to collect data, develop an Adoption Evaluation survey in which participants report their goal attainment. To minimize the likelihood of false-positives (people reporting successful adoption when in reality they have not adopted the behavior), one can survey the participant's manager also and only accept data when the manager and the participant agree on the level of goal attainment. To increase attainment, consider training participant's managers on what is supposed to happen after the course. The aim is that they know the goals and the anticipated behaviors after training.

A point to consider when developing your survey is to *keep it short*. Aim for a Web-based survey that can be completed in three to five minutes. The Adoption survey needs to capture the following data from participants:

- Demographics: these data are used to analyze results by organization, location, job function, etc. You also use these data to contact participants who are candidates for an Impact Evaluation survey and interview.

- Progress on each goal
- Work actually performed (the participant's Adoptive Behavior)
- Results from the performance
- Organizational elements that aided in goal completion
- Organizational elements that inhibited goal completion
- Current beliefs (optional)

A Web-based survey system is typically used to collect Adoption data. There are several survey tools available, such as Survey Monkey (www.surveymonkey .com) and Zoomerang (www.zoomerang.com), which are free or at a minimal cost, depending on the size of the respondent population.

Participant Demographics

Participant information, such as first name, last name, and e-mail address (so that you can identify and contact them if needed) are collected. With the name, you can also reference the participant's Intention Goals and Beliefs if necessary. Additional demographic data, such as organization, job function, location, etc., may be included in this section of the survey if needed.

Goal Progress

In this case, you are trying to find out what progress the participant has made on his or her goal. The survey questions in this section are as follows (from *Business Acumen Training*):

Question 1. Instructions: Find your goal sheet from Business Acumen Training and review your goals. During the training, you wrote business acumen leadership goals. What happened to your first goal?

- Completed: I do this all the time.
- Significant Progress: I do this most of the time.
- Some Progress: I tried a few times but gave up.
- No Progress: I did not put this goal into practice.
- No Recall: I forgot what my goal was.

The responses *Completed: I do this all the time* and *Significant Progress: I do this most of the time* are classified as successful adoption. The other three options are therefore participants who have not adopted. If participants choose one of the two successful statements, the survey branches to collect data on what they did, the result, and what helped them be successful.

Adoptive Behaviors and Enablers

Question 2. **What did you do?** Participants describe in their own words what work, tasks or actions they performed to implement their goal successfully. Successful adoption is not just self-reporting transference but also entails transferring the desired Adoptive Behaviors identified in the Impact Matrix.

Question 3. **What happened as a result?** The participant describes the outcomes from successful adoption. This is an early indicator of possible impact, and the data are used determine which participants, during Impact Evaluation, are surveyed and interviewed and which results are validated by examining company records.

Question 4. **What helped you implement this goal? (Check all that apply.)** This question seeks to uncover what factors (intrinsic or extrinsic) aided the participant in successful adoption. This is a typical list of enablers. You may add others or change as needed.

- I was motivated and wanted to make this change.
- My supervisor expected me to do this.
- My supervisor supported me in this goal.
- My team supported me in this goal.
- I had opportunities to put it into practice.
- Other; provide details.

Reasons for Non-Adoption

Question 5. **Give reasons why you made some or no progress. (Check all that apply.)** For participants who self-reported an unsuccessful adoption (*Some Progress, No Progress,* or *No Recall*), the survey branches to this question, which seeks to uncover what factors (intrinsic or extrinsic) inhibited the participant during adoption. This is a typical list of inhibitors. You may add others or change as needed.

- I have not had the opportunity to put it into practice.
- The pressure of work and/or lack of time made it difficult to implement my goal.
- My supervisor discouraged me from doing what I planned.
- My job changed, and so my goal is no longer relevant.
- I wasn't motivated enough to try.
- I lost my goal/forgot what my goal was.
- Other; provide details.

Beliefs during Adoption

Optionally, you can capture participant belief data during adoption; these are data that assess the extent to which key beliefs embedded in training are still held by participants some time after the training. If you choose to do this, use the same Belief statements from the Intention Evaluation and the same rating scale.

Question 6. **How meaningful are the following statements to you as a business leader?** During Intention Evaluation you measured the participant's beliefs. Now, a few months after graduation, you can capture the participant's beliefs to see if they have sustained the same results (believe the same), increased results (believe more), or decreased results (believe less). These data are useful in aiding in finding root causes that have enabled or inhibited adoption.

Steps for Designing a Good Survey

1. The first step in any survey is deciding what you want to learn. In our case, we want to learn goal progress, what was actually performed (adoptive behaviors), results from the work, enabling factors, inhibiting factors, and belief values.

2. Survey construction. Keep it simple. Ask yourself what you will do with the information from each question. If you cannot give yourself a satisfactory answer, leave out that question. Avoid the temptation to add a few more questions just because you are doing a survey anyway. If necessary, place your questions into three groups: must know, useful to know, and nice to know. Discard the last group unless the previous two groups are very short. Aim for a survey completion time of three to five minutes.

3. Pre-test the survey, if practical. The last step in survey design is to test it with a small number of participants before actual data collection begins. Ideally, you should test the survey on the same kinds of people you include in the evaluation. If that is not possible, have at least a few people other than the survey designer try the survey. This kind of test run can reveal unanticipated problems with question wording, instructions to skip questions, etc.

Step 3: Collect Adoption Data

When the Adoption survey has been designed and tested, determine the data collection period, sample size, and desired return rate. Figure 18 provides an example of an Adoption Evaluation data collection effort. In this scenario, the

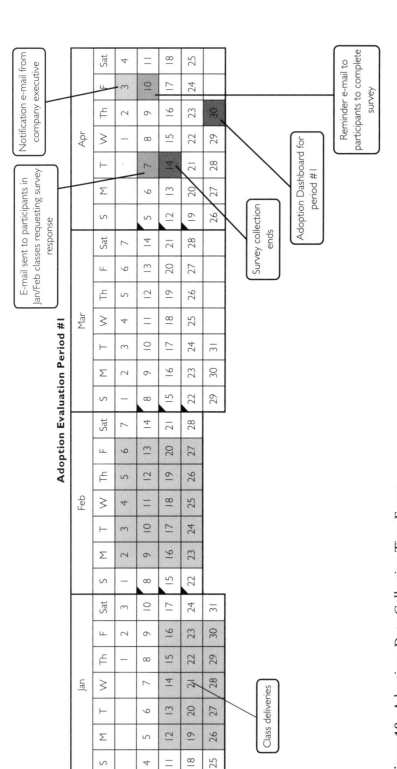

Figure 18: Adoptions Data Collection Time Frame

training program was delivered in January and February. Given the nature of the skills to be transferred, it was determined that a minimum of four weeks after graduation was needed for participants to implement their goals fully. Therefore, data collection needed to start four weeks after the final group of participants completed training.

The logistics involved in collecting Adoption data using a survey are as follows:

1. Arrange for an e-mail to the participants from a company executive notifying them to expect the survey the next week. It is a best practice to inform the participants before they leave the training that this evaluation will be occurring.

2. On the appointed date, the same company executive has an e-mail sent to the participants requesting them to complete the Adoptions survey. Suggestion: write the e-mail for them and get them to approve it. Note: you may get a higher return rate if the e-mail comes from the participants' direct executive (e.g., Vice President of Sales) rather than from the CEO. The following e-mail content that has been successful in achieving a high return:

   Subject: ATTENTION REQUIRED: three-minute survey

   XYZ Company is conducting an evaluation of the [training program name] that you attended in January or February.

   The survey has three questions only and will take you approximately three to five minutes to complete. At a later date, some of you will be contacted for additional feedback. Your input will help identify how we can reinforce success or improve what is not working well with this program.

   Although your contact information will be captured, only the external evaluators will see it. Absolutely no individual survey data will be released to any supervisor or any other individual in the company. No one will be identified in any way in the evaluation report.

   Click here: [survey_link_goes_here].

   Please complete by [date goes here].

   Any questions or concerns can be sent to [evaluator name] at [evaluator e-mail].

3. Four days after the e-mail initiating data collection, a reminder e-mail is sent from the company executive reminding participants to complete the survey.

4. Data collection concludes after one week, although it may pay to keep the survey open for two more days after the announced end date in order to pick up late responders.

Data Collection Rate

In order to generalize from the data to the entire participant population, you must get a minimum number of responses. The minimum depends on the size of the population of participants. Many evaluation textbooks provide details about how to calculate this minimum number, but a simple explanation is provided here.

Population: in an Adoption Evaluation, this refers to all who have attended the training program. In the example on the previous page, it is everyone who completed class in January and February.

Sample size: the portion of the population to be surveyed. For example, if you had 5,000 people, that is your population. However, your sample size would probably be about 500. You certainly wouldn't want to be collecting Adoption data from all 5,000. Consult a book or other reference to find out how to calculate the sample size based on the number of usable responses you must have, or see Figure 19. So if you need 100 usable responses and you think you'll be lucky to get more than 30 percent return rate, your sample needs to be 300 out of 5,000.

Confidence level: The confidence level tells you how sure you can be. It is expressed as a percentage and represents how often the true percentage of the population who pick an answer lies within the confidence interval. A 95 percent confidence level means you can be 95 percent certain that the conclusions you draw are real; the 99 percent confidence level means you can be 99 percent certain. It is recommended that you use a minimum 95 percent confidence level for Adoption Evaluation.

Confidence interval: This is usually expressed as +/– 10 percent or +/– 5 percent, and represents the level of confidence that an evaluator has in the accuracy of the data as representative of how the entire population would have responded. A confidence level of 5 percent requires a much higher percentage of total population response than a 10 percent confidence level does. If there is a confidence interval of 5 and 47 percent of the participants selected response "c" to a multiple-choice question, you can be confident that between 42 percent (47 – 5) and 52 percent (47 + 5) of the participants would have picked the same answer. For an Adoption Evaluation, try to use a confidence interval of 5 percent, but recognize that in many evaluations it is not possible to get the high rate of return that is needed and that you may have to settle for a 10 percent confidence interval.

An excellent site to help you determine all of this is at
www.surveysystem.com/sscalc.htm.

So what does all of this mean in an Adoption Evaluation? An example
will demonstrate. A survey is e-mailed to 1,000 participants, and the evaluator wants enough responses to be at the 95 percent confidence level. What is
the number of completed surveys (return rate) necessary to be at the 95 percent confidence level? **Answer: 278.** That is a 27.8 percent response rate. If
there are fewer than 278 responses, the evaluator will not be able to generalize from the data and draw conclusions about the entire population of participants (see Figure 19). This chart shows how the response rate varies based
on the population/sample size and on response rate charts found in many statistics books.

Adoption Evaluation Survey Return Rate Chart at 95% confidence level with a confidence interval of 5		
Population/Sample Size	**Return Rate**	**# of Completed Surveys**
20	95%	19
30	93%	28
40	90%	36
50	88%	44
60	87%	52
70	84%	59
80	83%	66
90	81%	73
100	80%	80
200	66%	132
300	56%	169
400	49%	196
500	43%	217
750	34%	254
1,000	28%	278
1,500	20%	306
2,000	16%	322
2,500	13%	333

Figure 19: Adoption Survey Return Rate

Step 4: Calculate Adoption Rate and Compare against Success Gate

Adoption Data Record Structure

After you have collected Adoption data via the survey, the next step is to calculate the rate of adoption. Adoption data are organized into a data structure with one record per participant. A typical Adoption data structure is as follows:

- Participant Demographic
  - First name
  - Last name
  - E-mail

- Goal Performance
  - Goal number
  - Progress
    - Completed
    - Significant
    - Some progress
    - No progress
    - Cannot recall goal
  - What did you do?
  - What happened as a result?
  - Enabler(s)
  - Inhibitor(s)

- Belief 1 rating

- Belief 2 rating

- Belief n rating

Next, data are sorted, interpreted, and conclusions drawn in order to determine if Adoption has occurred as predicted. Collected data must be properly managed and stored in preparing for analysis. In some cases, you may question the accuracy and completeness of collected data. The following questions will help in this case.

- Are responses complete? If not, should the incomplete ones be kept or rejected?

- Have any of the data been contaminated?

- Have there been data entry errors? A data entry specialist may make errors when inputting data into a system. Check entries and correct errors.

- Are respondents a representative sample of the population? For example, in a global evaluation, how significant is it if there is very little response from Asia, which accounts for 20 percent of the training population?

- Is the response rate high enough to provide the level of statistical confidence you require? If not, you may want to send out a reminder to encourage more to respond, or you may have to work with data that does not meet your confidence level and therefore cannot be generalized to the entire training population.

- Have data collection administrative procedures been implemented as planned?

- Are there a high number of responses that indicate a poorly developed survey (e.g., an ambiguous question that elicited two different types of responses depending on how it was interpreted)? If so, consider whether that question should not be included in the data.

Use a spreadsheet or database to summarize survey data.

Steps to Analyze Adoption Data

1. Download survey results into a spreadsheet or database.

2. Determine how many participants have successful adoption by reviewing the records where participants have self-reported successful adoption (*Completed* or *Significant Progress*). Read each description of the work performed and see if it matches (or is similar to) any of the Adoptive Behaviors on the Impact Matrix. If, in your opinion, it does match, code that participant as *Successful Adoption*. If collected data cannot be matched to an Adoptive Behavior, code that participant as *Unsuccessful Adoption*. At times, participants are reporting on multiple goals. Judge each goal. Participants are classified as *Successful Adoption* if any one of their goals is successful. If no goals are successful, participants are classified as *Unsuccessful Adoption*.

3. Sort the data by Adoptive Behavior and calculate the Adoption Rate per behavior. To calculate Adoption Rate, count the number of participants who have been coded as successful and divide by the total number of participants who responded for that behavior. The resulting percentage is the Adoption Rate. Do this for each behavior. Figure 20 shows the results for Business Acumen Training.

4. Summarize the enabling and inhibiting of factors.

	Predicted Adoption Rate	# of Participants with Successful Adoption	Total Participants Reporting on the Behavior	Actual Adoption Rate	Successful Adoption? (Y/N)
• **AB1:** Obtain and enhance VOC for existing and potential customers.	50%	90	120	75%	Y
• **AB2:** Develop products/ services roadmaps aligned with the goals of the customer while maximizing recurring revenue opportunity	60%	10	50	29%	N
• **AB3:** Facilitate sessions with their team, discussing with them the ways in which they help to improve key financial metrics.	50%	60	85	71%	Y
• **AB4:** Lay out planned activities and corresponding monetary resources for the fiscal year, including recurring annual expenses and nonrecurring investments in special projects.	35%	15	65	23%	N
N = 342 participants					

Figure 20: Business Acumen Training Adoption Rates

Step 5: Create Adoption Dashboard

An Adoption Dashboard is a vehicle for showing evaluation data in a few pages and provides insight into the success of training and whether it is reaching its predicted Adoption results. The Adoption Dashboard (Figures 21–24) is typically four pages in length and comprises the following.

Page 1: Adoption and Belief Results

Adoption results are depicted in a bar graph that shows the percentage of participants who have achieved successful adoption and those who have not by Adoptive Behavior. The Adoption Rate Success Gate is shown as a reference point for each behavior.

Optional data that can be collected during an Adoption Evaluation are the participant's belief statements. Belief results are shown on the dashboard in a data table. The purpose is to capture belief data in order to see to what degree participant belief data has changed since training. It may be trending up, because, as participants master their skills, they believe more. This is similar to members of a sports team that starts the season and, as they work together and win games, their belief that they can win increases. Successful adoption may have the same effect in this case.

Belief data may be trending down. There are two possible explanations for this. One is that end-of-course results reflect the high experienced at the end of excellent training—some overrating may be occurring. Another is that the end-of-course beliefs have been impacted by the reality of the workplace. In other words, participants have found that there is not as much opportunity or support to act in empowered ways as they had believed.

Page 2: Detailed Adoption Results; Enablers and Inhibitors to Adoption

This page contains a table that shows the detailed Adoption results by Adoptive Behavior. The number of responses and associated percentage are shown for each of the goal progress statements. The data are converted into the percentage of Successful Adoption participants and the Unsuccessful Adoption ones. The predicted Adoption Rate Success Gate is shown so that the reader can determine whether Adoptive Behavior has been successfully implemented.

Also shown are the environmental and individual factors that have enabled and inhibited adoption. Survey design captures enabling factors when participants choose Completed or Significant Progress as their goal progress. If participants choose Some Progress, No Progress, or No Recall as their goal progress,

Adoption Dashboard Page 1

Adoption Results

Adoptive Behaviors

AB1: Obtain and enhance VOC for existing and potential customers.

AB2: Develop products/services roadmaps aligned with the goals of the customer while maximizing recurring revenue opportunity.

AB3: Facilitate sessions with their team, discussing with them the ways in which they help to improve key financial metrics.

AB4: Lay out planned activities and corresponding monetary resources for the fiscal year, including recurring annual expenses and nonrecurring investments in special projects.

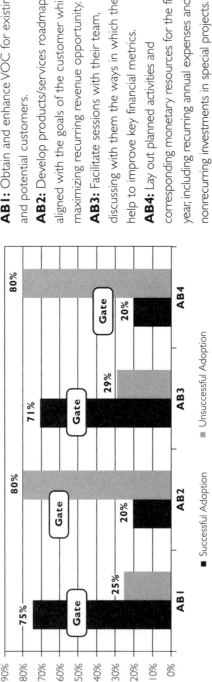

■ Successful Adoption   ▓ Unsuccessful Adoption

Belief Score: % rating 6 or 7 (1 = meaningless, 7 = meaningful)	
85%	Business leaders must operate with a customer-centric focus.
55%	Customer intimacy is a transformative strategy that results in improved sales, service, and overall satisfaction.
92%	Successful execution of strategy is a function of thinking, planning, action, and learning.
92%	Use of appropriate metrics drive accountability and results.
89%	Innovation is a key to sustainable and profitable growth.

Figure 21: Adoption Dashboard, Page 1

Adoption Dashboard Page 2

N = 342 participants	AB1		AB2		Survey Response Rate = 59% AB3		AB4	
	No.	%	No.	%	No.	%	No.	%
Completed	100	34%	10	11%	20	18%	5	7%
Significant Progress	120	41%	8	9%	60	53%	9	13%
Some Progress	50	17%	45	49%	18	16%	32	45%
No Progress	17	6%	20	22%	15	13%	20	28%
No Recall	5	2%	8	9%	0	0%	5	7%
Total Participants	292		91		113		71	
Success Gate	50%		60%		50%		35%	
Successful	75%		20%		71%		20%	
Unsuccessful	25%		80%		29%		80%	

Enabling Factors	AB1		AB2		AB3		AB4	
	No.	%	No.	%	No.	%	No.	%
I was motivated and wanted to make this change	42	23%	12	33%	90	51%	12	29%
My supervisor expected me to do this	40	22%	4	11%	6	3%	0	0%
My supervisor supported me in this goal	18	10%	8	22%	22	13%	3	7%
My team supported me in this goal	12	7%	4	11%	12	7%	0	0%
I had opportunities to put it into practice	40	22%	8	22%	40	23%	24	59%
Other	28	16%	0	0%	5	3%	2	5%
Total Participants	180		36		175		41	

Inhibiting Factors	AB1		AB2		AB3		AB4	
	No.	%	No.	%	No.	%	No.	%
I have not had the opportunity to put it into practice	6	5%	4	25%	44	46%	0	0%
The pressure of work and/or lack of time made it difficult to implement my goal	50	39%	2	13%	32	33%	2	20%
My supervisor discourged me from doing what I planned	8	6%	0	0%	4	4%	0	0%
My job changed and so my goal is no longer relevant	15	12%	0	0%	2	2%	0	0%
I wasn't motivated enough to try	14	11%	0	0%	4	4%	3	30%
I lost my goal/forgot what my goal was	36	28%	8	50%	2	2%	4	40%
Other	0	0%	2	13%	8	8%	1	10%
Total Participants	129		16		96		10	

Figure 22: Adoption Dashboard, Page 2

Adoption Dashboard Page 3

Examples of Adoptive Behaviors

What did you do?	What happened as a result?
Found my company's P-E Ratio, Market-to-Book Ratio, and Total Shareholder Return. Compared our ratios with those of our competitors. Discussed with my team some possible reasons for the differences in the magnitudes of these ratios between our competitors and our company.	Nothing as of yet, but I hope to increase the value we create for shareholders, and my team understands how we contribute to and affect total shareholder return.
Reviewed the types of assets used by my operation. Evaluated which assets are more important in terms of operations and monetary value. Identified which assets I have responsibility for purchasing and/or utilizing.	I have increased my Total Asset Turnover ratio from 1.78 to 2.10.

Figure 23: Adoption Dashboard, Page 3

Adoption Dashboard Page 4

Evaluator Comments

- 2 of the 4 Adoptive Behaviors have been successfully implemented.

- 342 participants reported 567 Adoptive Behaviors (some respondents had 2 behaviors).

- The response rate is 59%—more than acceptable for a survey.

- Interviews are currently being scheduled with a number of respondents who report successful implementation of their goals, in order to determine the impact on the company and better understand the reasons for their successful outcome from the training.

- All respondents who responded "I *did not try to put this goal into practice*" are being interviewed to identify the reasons why, and to find out whether program modifications could reduce this number in the future.

- Pressure of work has increased significantly since the last evaluation as a stated reason for failure to implement the end of course goals. This does not necessarily mean, however, that these individuals have not changed their work behavior to align with the safety practices taught on the course.

Figure 24: Adoption Dashboard, Page 4

they are asked to provide the inhibitors. Note: the survey allows participants to choose as many enablers and inhibitors as they feel warranted.

Page 3: Examples of Adoptive Behavior

It is important for the dashboard reader to get a sense of what performance is happening on-the-job as a result of training. From the Adoption, select three to six relevant samples and display them on this page.

Page 4: Evaluator Comments

Because you, as the evaluator, have poured over the data, you have the best sense of what it means. Therefore, use this page to convey your findings, conclusions, and recommendations.

Figures 21–24 show the complete Adoption Dashboard for Business Acumen Training.

Step 5: Analyze and React

Actions taken at this point are dictated by whether or not Adoption has been successful. When analyzing Adoptions data, consider the following questions:

- How much progress has been made to date?
- Has the Success Gate been met?
- What has been the value (tangible business result) of goal adoption?
- What elements in the work environment have enabled goal adoption?
- What elements have hindered goal adoption?
- Are adopted goals in alignment with the course's desired outcomes?
- Have unforeseen (positive and negative) outcomes been reported? For example, in one program, the data clearly pointed toward a shift in company culture that was contributing to successful adoption, although this was not an intended outcome in the course design.

You now need to determine whether the training has had successful adoption. Look at each of the Adoptive Behaviors reported by participants and compare them to the Impact Matrix. Do actual behaviors match those defined in the Matrix? How does the actual Adoption Rate compare to the rate on the Matrix? Are you seeing behaviors that were not predicted but that seem appropriate?

If the Adoption Rate Success Gate has been reached or exceeded, no corrective actions are needed. Determine what factors, if any, have significantly contributed to the success and draw conclusions. If the Success Gate has not been met, review the data and prepare suggestions (action items) that the company may consider to increase adoption.

Next, analyze the Belief results. Are they trending up or down from the results collected during Intention Evaluation? Why is this? What conclusions, if any, can you draw?

Reviewing both Adoption and Belief results, write one paragraph describing what you have found. What are the data telling you? What recommendations would you make to sustain excellent results? What recommendations would you make improve results?

Adoption Evaluation and Continuous Improvement

A variety of activities can be implemented to improve adoption if results are below the Success Gate. Consider implementing some of the following activities listed:

- Assign internal coaches to participants.
- Implement formal and informal mentoring programs.
- Supply a post-program tool and technique handbook for on-the-job use.
- Conduct virtual retreats with a cohort of participants.
- Create an online community for the co-creation of application suggestions and sharing. Use tools such as Wiki's, blogs, online forums, chat rooms, threaded discussions, and cross-business unit forums.
- Provide a roadmap: give participants guidance on how to best practice their new skills and knowledge until they achieve adoption.
- Educate participants' managers on program goals and provide them with tools to provide support, feedback, and reinforcement of the proper skills and application.
- Conduct a pre-program teleconference with managers and provide them with information on the training, its goals, and predicted business impact.
- Encourage managers to meet with participants, pre- and post-program, to agree on goals and results that the participant should focus on and need to achieve their business objectives.

- Develop and distribute a coaching guide for managers that documents the following: (1) what was taught (new capabilities), (2) what a participant can do on the job with the new capabilities, and (3) tips on coaching and supporting their employee.

If there is one thing that the literature on transfer is very clear about, it is that perception of supervisor support influences adoption. Although most participants believe personal motivation is the key factor in whether or not they use the training on-the-job and that the support of their supervisor has no influence on their performance, this is not the case. Assuming training content is relevant to the job, the perception of supervisor support influences transfer significantly more than any other factor.

A second influential factor is accountability. In other words, when participants go to training knowing they have to give an account in some way, it increases their engagement with the material, and the reporting back (giving account) contributes to higher adoption levels.

Setting expectations about what an individual should focus on is also important. Often a supervisor knows better than the participants what skills or knowledge they should focus on. Or it may be that the supervisor sees an overall weak area in the team and wants the participants to help develop that area using what they learn in the training program. By communicating expectations, the supervisor is focusing the participants on those aspects of the content that are most useful on-the-job.

When participants enter a class with only a vague understanding (or worse, a misunderstanding) of what the training is about, valuable learning time is lost while they get oriented. In addition, they may be demotivated initially, based on what they understand about the content, and fail to engage with the training content for the first few hours. It is critical that participants arrive at a class knowing what the content covers, why they are there, what they can expect to learn, and how it can improve their performance.

You can increase the likelihood of adoption by implementing three activities:

1. Pre-course conversations between the participants and their supervisor

2. Intention Evaluation goal planning by participants while in training

3. Post-course goal formalization and ongoing support

Pre-Course Conversation

During training, many participants feel overwhelmed by the quantity of information presented to them. A pre-course conversation between the participants and their supervisors helps them focus on the content that is relevant to them, their team, and/or the company. Training departments are often reluctant to ask supervisors to do "one more thing." Providing a pre-course conversation job aid for supervisors makes this approach as easy and as focused as possible. Experience has shown that spending just a few minutes with participants before training makes a significant difference in what the participants focus on.

The pre-course conversation need not be extensive and can be done in person or via phone. A job aid to guide supervisors ensures that they hold a fruitful conversation. Figure 25 is an example of a job aid for Business Acumen Training.

Post-Course Conversation Job Aid

Holding a brief conversation with participants after training makes a significant difference in what gets applied on-the-job, especially if supervisors review participants' goals. Figure 26 is an example of a job aid for this conversation.

Goal Formalization

Whenever possible, managers need to formalize employees' learning goal(s) by entering them into the company's Performance Management System. This allows managers to monitor goal progress. Goal formalization can focus the performance and provide management with some sense of the overall activities involved in the effort. Goals should be clear enough so that success can be recognized when it occurs (use the SOS + D model whenever possible).

Coaching Guide for Supervisors

You can significantly increase individual and team productivity by providing participants with ongoing support and coaching after training. Coaching/support may be provided by the participant's supervisor, a colleague, or a mentor. Effective coaching is timely and relevant to what has been learned. The coach helps employees meet their training goals and improve certain areas of performance.

Outline for Effective Coaching

- Let participants know what's expected; clearly define job duties, responsibilities, and the standards for achievement.
- Translate what was learned in class to on-the-job behaviors.
- Help participants implement the plan to achieve their Intention Goals.
- Observe performance and improvement.
- Praise improvement: encourage new efforts.

Business Acumen **Pre-course Conversation Job Aid**

In a few days, one of your employees will be attending *Business Acumen*. The company requires that you, as the supervisor, have a 5-minute conversation with your employee to discuss the upcoming class. The goal of this process is to increase transfer by setting learning expectations, communicating accountability to your employee, and providing your support during and after class.

When you meet with your employee before they attend class, have the following conversation.
Provide a high-level background briefing (things you may say …)

- The reason for this class is to (1) use financial analysis to maintain fiscal discipline and to make sound business decisions, (2) recognize revenue and profit potential in business opportunities, and (3) manage a business's overall financial performance (balance sheet, income statement, and cash flow statement).

- We need leaders to drive top-line growth of 8%–12% and net profit margin of 7%.

- Topic areas/content blocks in *Business Acumen* are
  - How to Read a Financial Report
  - Key Financial Indicators
  - Cash Flow
  - Managerial and Cost Accounting

Write your own notes here: _____
_____
_____

- *Expectation: What are you going to bring back to drive top-line growth* and *net profit margin?* (things you may say …)

- What areas would like to work on? (Note: you as the supervisor may suggest an area that you want the employee to focus on.) Come to agreement on one or two areas (refer to the topic areas/content block listed above). Things to think about: How will this drive top-line growth and net profit margin?

- Inform the employee of your expectation to hold a post-training discussion to talk about their goals and how you will suport them.

Write your own notes here: _____
_____
_____

Figure 25: Pre-Course Conversation Job Aid

Business Acumen **Post-course Conversation Job Aid**

Within a week upon completing *Business Acumen,* have a 5–10 minute conversation on with your employee to discuss/refine their goal(s) and establish a mechanism for supporting their efforts (things you may say . . .)

- Look at the employee's goals and discuss them. Do you agree these are the best goals for them? Do they need fine-tuning? Get agreement on goals.
- Ask: What kind of help do you need to make these goals happen?
- Who do you need help from—me? Others?
- How will we know we are making progress?
- Set a check-in date to review goal progress.

Note: Check your employee's goals with the course purpose of driving top-line growth of 8%–12% and net profit margin of 7%. Ensure that the work to be performed will contribute to these results.

Write your own notes here: _____

_____

_____

Figure 26: Post-Course Conversation Job Aid

- Secure help from others as necessary.
- Constructively correct failures.
- Teach by example.
- Periodically review process.
- Provide participants with meaningful and regular feedback in performance.

Supervisors often need help in how to coach the right things to achieve the training's desired results. A Coaching Guide written specifically for the course focuses the supervisor's effort to support the proper Adoptive Behaviors. For each major section of course content, the guide should supply three elements:

- What was taught (new capabilities)
- What employees can do on-the-job with the new capabilities (these are the Adoption Behaviors that the evaluation measures)
- Tips on how to coach and support employees

Adoption Evaluation Summary

An Adoption Evaluation addresses the following question: *How much of the training has been implemented on-the-job and successfully integrated into the participants' work behavior?* It analyzes and evaluates participant goal completion (Adoptive Behavior) against a defined Adoption Success Gate. As with an Intention Evaluation, an Adoption Dashboard is produced, and, if needed, corrective actions are put in place to improve the rate of adoption. When the right Adoptive Behaviors are implemented by participants, the likelihood of improving business and organizational results is increased.

Chapter 5

Impact Evaluation

Impact Evaluation is identifying the direct impact on and value to the business that can be traced to training. It assesses in quantifiable terms the value of the training by assessing what Adoptive Behaviors have made a measurable difference. Impact evaluation goes beyond assessing the degree to which participants are using what was learned; it provides a reliable and valid measure of the results of the training to the organization.

When participants report a positive impact from training, this approach allows you to articulate how and why training is impacting the business, with a view to leveraging this information to enhance the organizational impact of future deliveries. Conversely, when little or no impact is found, this evaluation method uncovers why that is so and what can be done to remedy that undesirable outcome.

Impact evaluation seeks value to the business. This is done by collecting data on actual business results that participants attribute to successful adoption of their Intention Goal(s). In their Adoption Evaluation survey, participants told us what they did, and we classified them as *Successful Adoption* or *Unsuccessful Adoption*. From the successful participants, you now collect additional impact data via three methods: (1) completion of an Impact Survey, (2) interviewing participants, and (3) examination of company records to confirm findings. The steps to conducting a successful Impact Evaluation are the following:

Step 1: Develop the Impact Survey

Step 2: Collect Detailed Impact Data from Successful Participants

Step 3: Analyze Survey Data

Step 4: Interview Successful and Unsuccessful Participants

Step 5: Collect Impact Data from Company Records

Step 6: Create Impact Dashboard and Evaluation Report

Step 1: Develop the Impact Survey

Adoption Evaluation, as an output, sorts participants into either *Successful Adoption* or *Unsuccessful Adoption*. Participants labeled *Successful* needed to meet two criteria: (1) self-reporting successful implementation of their Intention

Goal and (2) what they did matches an Adoptive Behavior on the Impact Matrix. These are the participants most likely to have results, and you want to more information from them on that impact. You do this via an Impact Survey. The Impact Survey is like the scorecard of results. From the participants, you want it to capture the following:

- Details on the performance: what they did, what tools and techniques they used
- Results realized from that performance: what impact has occurred (cost savings, higher production, less defects, increased sales, etc.)
- Where claimed results can be validated
- Percentage by which training provided the impact
- Whether the impact is sustainable and repeatable
- Percentage by which other factors (external or internal to the company) contributed to the impact

The survey needs to collect enough data from participants so that you can analyze the results and compare them to the predicted impact (found in the training's Impact Matrix). A good starting point is to review the Impact Matrix and use it as your guide for the survey. Let's look at the Impact Survey from Business Acumen Training.

Impact Survey General Information

- First Name
- Last Name
- E-mail

This is the demographic data for the Impact Survey.

Results per Adoptive Behavior

Impact data are collected for each Adoptive Behavior so that you can generalize the results and compare them to the predicted value on the Impact Matrix. The same set of questions is asked for each behavior. The flow of the survey is as follows:

1. Present the Adoptive Behavior (from the Impact Matrix) to participants.
2. Ask whether or not they have done something similar to the listed behavior. If yes, have them complete the questions for that behavior. If no, branch to the next behavior and repeat the process.

Adoptive Behavior Results Questions

Section Header. **In Business Acumen, you learned how to obtain and enhance VOC for existing and potential customers. Please answer the following questions with respect to this.** This header statement focuses participants on a given Adoptive Behavior. In this case, *obtain and enhance VOC for existing and potential customers.* The behavior is pulled directly from the Impact Matrix, and the questions are for that behavior. You create one page like this for each behavior in the survey.

1. **Did you do something similar to this? If yes, continue with the remaining questions on this page. If no, continue to the next page. [Yes/No].** This is the filter question (determines whether or not participants continue with this section of the survey). If participants' on-the-job performance is similar to the behavior, they respond yes and continue with the questions for this behavior. If their work is not similar to the behavior, they respond no and the survey branches to the next behavior.

2. **Describe what you did. Be as specific as possible.** Here you want a complete description of the work actually performed. These data are examined to see what actually has transferred to the workplace. An example from Business Acumen Training for the VOC adoptive behavior was this: *"For the Walnut Locking residential series, I identified a hierarchical set of 'customer needs' where each need had an assigned priority that indicated its importance to the customer. My first use of the VOC was in positioning. By understanding the dimensions of competition, we were able to identify how to differentiate our brand to achieve a 0.5 percent growth in sales. One of those needs was electronic Keypad Entry Locks and Deadbolts with no keys to hide, lose, carry, or forget. That feature was introduced to the marketplace in Q1 for this line of products."*

3. **What was the business result from doing this?** This question seeks tangible results from participants' efforts and are a direct output of the work performed. Continuing with the example from BAT, *"Following product launch, we saw a 0.7 percent increase in sales for the Walnut line."*

4. **What dollar value resulted from this? Please enter a value or "none at this time" if you do not have any.** This question captures the monetary value from the business result identified in question 3. The participants enter the value, or, if they have no monetary value,

they enter "none at this time." Continuing with our BAT example, the participant wrote: *"The increase in sales so far has produced an additional $2,500 in revenue."*

5. **How long did it take you get this result?** These data tell you the length it took the participant to produce the result and corresponding value. Analysis of the data tells you whether participants are performing at the proper pace or not. When deciding on anchors, review the Impact Matrix and select responses that are appropriate for that Adoptive Behavior. For this BAT example, the choices were the following:
   – One month
   – One quarter
   – Six months
   – Longer than six months

6. **Is this result sustainable? (Will you continue the action that produced this result?) [Yes/No].** Here you are trying to find out if the result will be ongoing—whether it will continue and produce the impact time and time again.

7. **Where can these results be validated? Please list company records.** These data will assist you later in validating results claimed by participants.

8. **What percentage did the use of skills and knowledge from Business Acumen Training contribute to these results?** If this value is low, you could assume that the impact would have occurred naturally if the participant had not been trained. A high value indicates that training had a significant impact on the results.

9. **Did the CRM system contribute to these results? [Yes/No].** Here you are trying to assess the external contribution factors on the impact. **If yes, what percentage of the result did it contribute?** If the response to question 9 is yes, capture the contribution as a percentage of results for this factor.

   Reference the Impact Matrix and list the external and internal forces that the Steering Committee predicted and produce one question per factor.

10. **Did anything else contribute to these results? [Yes/No].** At times, other factors not identified by the Steering Committee have contributed to the results. This question captures these factors. **If yes, what was it? What percentage of these results did it contribute to?**
    As with all surveys, pre-test with potential respondents and modify as necessary.

Step 2: Collect Detailed Impact Data from Successful Participants

Prior to sending the survey, it is a good idea to build the *data analysis model* that used to summarize the data. It usually takes the form of a spreadsheet or database. In a spreadsheet, the data structure in each row is one participant response with the columns being the data.

Impact Data Structure

A typical data structure for Impact Survey data is the following:

- Participant Demographic
  - First name
  - Last name
  - E-mail
- Impact Data (repeat for each behavior)
  - Adoptive Behavior number
  - Was this done? [Yes/No]
  - Description of work performed
  - Business result
  - Dollar value
  - Length to accomplish work
  - Result sustainable [Yes/No]
  - Where results can be validated
  - Percentage by which training skills and knowledge contributed to results
  - Factor 1 contribution [Yes/No]
  - Factor 1 contribution, percentage
  - Factor 2 contribution [Yes/No]
  - Factor 2 contribution, percentage
  - Factor n contribution [Yes/No]
  - Factor n contribution, percentage

Survey Administration

With the survey fully tested and the data structure prepared, begin administering the Impact Survey to all participants classified as *Successful Adoption* from the Adoption Evaluation. Draft an e-mail from a company executive soliciting survey completion and watch the response rate (the ratio of number of people who answered the survey divided by the number of people in the sample, usually expressed in the form of a percentage). A reminder e-mail is sent requesting completion of the survey. You want to get the highest return rate as possible, because obtaining a high response rate can bolster statistical power, reduce sampling error, and enhance the generalizability of the results to the population (participants). Refer to Chapter 4 for information on return rate and confidence level.

When to collect data is a factor of the number of course deliveries and volume of participants trained. Other guidelines on the timing or frequency of data collection include the following:

- Intention Evaluation: collect at the conclusion of each course. For classroom courses, collect a goal sheet from each participant. For e-learning courses, embed the goal sheet into the end-of-course programming and submit it to the data analysis model.

- Adoption Evaluation: collect data when a sufficient number of participants have graduated and have had the opportunity to transfer their skills to the workplace. If you have a sufficient population size, you do not have to collect adoption data from all participants. Collect enough data to ensure a reasonable return rate and sample to obtain a high degree of confidence.

- Impact Evaluation: collect data immediately after the Adoption data have been analyzed and reported.

Let's look at an example for a year-long data collection effort for a two-day leadership course that has ten to fifteen deliveries each month for 200 to 300 participants. Intention data collection was at the end of each class. After reviewing the skills taught, it was determined that participants needed four weeks to practice their new skills before Adoption data collection could begin. This resulted in collecting data three times over the course of the year for two months of participants. This provided a sample size with a return rate to achieve a 95 percent confidence level. Note: it was not necessary to evaluate all participants in order to draw accurate conclusions for the entire population.

Impact data collection (survey, interviews, and company record retrieval) was conducted for the participants labeled *Successful Adoption* from the Adoption Evaluation. It also was done three times in the year immediately following the Adoption Evaluation. This too provided a sufficient sample to draw conclusions at the 95 percent confidence level.

Data Scrubbing

When collection has ceased, you need to scrub the Impact data. Data scrubbing, sometimes, called data cleansing, is the process of detecting and removing or correcting any information in a database (or spreadsheet) that has some sort of error. This error can be because the data are wrong, incomplete, formatted incorrectly, or are a duplicate copy of another entry (the participant responded multiple times). Simply review the data and make the necessary corrections.

Step 3: Analyze Survey Data[1]

In this step, the data are sorted and interpreted and conclusions are drawn in order to answer the evaluation questions: *What impact has the company received from training? How does that impact compare to predicted impact?*

Quantitative Data Analysis

For quantitative data, use the data analysis model and prepare appropriate descriptive statistics, charts, and graphs. The statistics, charts, and graphs for an Impact Evaluation are simple, and the best way to show this is by reviewing the results from Business Acumen Training.

Question 1: Did you do something similar to this? If yes, continue with the remaining questions on this page. If no, continue to the next page. [Yes/No]. The best statistic for this question is a relative comparison shown as a percentage. Note: always include the number of responses that make up the data.

Adoptive Behavior: **obtain and enhance Voice of Customer for existing and potential customers.**	
Response (n = 342)	Percentage
Yes	38%
No	62%

This is telling us that 38 percent (125 participants) of the 342 respondents have tried something similar to obtaining and enhancing Voice of Customer for existing and potential customers.

Question 2: Describe what you did. Be as specific as possible. With data such as these, you perform a qualitative data analysis. For qualitative data, read through the data. This is where raw data are ordered and organized so that useful information can be extracted from them. The process of organizing and thinking about data is key to understanding what data do and do not contain. Make notes of the patterns and themes that emerge from the data. Answer these questions:

1. What are the data telling you?

2. What is missing?

3. What are the central themes contained in the data?

4. Are you uncovering something unexpected? What is it? Is it pertinent to the evaluation?

A simple way to analyze qualitative Impact data (this can also be applied to qualitative Adoption data) is to code and segment the data. First, carefully read the data, line by line, and divide the data into meaningful segments (logical groupings). When you locate meaningful segments, code them. For example, for the conduct Voice of Customer (VOC) Adoptive Behavior from BAT, some of the codes created to represent the work performed were the following:

- VOC surveys

- VOC focus groups

- VOC market research

- VOC interviews

- VOC customer service feedback

After you finish the initial coding of your data, attempt to summarize and organize the data. You also continue to refine and revise your codes. Count the number of times a code appears in order to give you an idea of the frequency of the code.

Next, you want to look for relationships within the coded data. For example, are participants from a business unit doing more of a code than others? Are more experienced participants performing differently than inexperienced ones? What relationship exists, if any, between such things as job role and impact data, tenure and impact data, or external factors and impact data? For visually oriented people, creating a drawing or a sketch of the relationships often helps.

Stepping back and looking at the summarized coded data and any relationships among the data, you can draw conclusions. There are a variety of ways in which you can approach data analysis, and it is easy to manipulate the data unintentionally to support desired conclusions or agendas. For this reason, it is important to pay attention when data are analyzed and to think critically about the data and the conclusions to be drawn.

Question 3: What was the business result from doing this? These also are qualitative data that are coded, frequencies counted, and relationships drawn. Here you are looking for the common business results from performing the action defined in question 2.

Question 4: What dollar value resulted from this? Please enter a value or "none at this time" if you do not have any. This is quantitative data analysis because of the data themselves (a dollar value), and, with data of this nature, you usually use measures of central tendency. Measures of central tendency describe the center of the data.

- Mean: arithmetic average
- Median: middle value
- Mode: most common response

Measures of variability can also be used with this data type; they describe the spread of the data.

- High value
- Low value
- Range: distance between the highest and lowest scores
- Standard deviation: average distance of every score from the mean

For example, for BAT's Impact Evaluation, the following chart shows measures of variability.

Adoptive Behavior: **obtain and enhance VOC for existing and potential customers.**

Response (n = 125)	Value
Mean	$3,400
Median	$4,000
Mode	$4,000
High value	$7,000
Low value	$0
Range	$7,000
Standard Deviation	$1,500

Looking at these results, you can conclude that Impact is being realized with an average value of $4,000. The standard deviation is kind of the "mean of the mean," and it can often help you find the story behind the data. To understand this concept, it can help to learn about what statisticians call normal distribution of data. A normal distribution of data means that most of the examples in a set of data are close to the average, whereas relatively few examples tend to one extreme or the other. The standard deviation is a statistic that tells you how tightly all the various examples are clustered around the mean in a set of data. When the examples are pretty tightly bunched together and the bell-shaped curve is steep, the standard deviation is small. When the examples are spread apart and the bell curve is relatively flat, you have a relatively large standard deviation.

Typically, two-thirds of the values fall within +1 and −1 standard deviations from the mean. In our BAT example, with a mean of $4,000 and a standard deviation of $1,500, you can conclude that two-thirds of the Impact realized is between $2,500 and $5,000. That's not bad, given that the training's Impact Map predicted an impact of $5,000 for this Adoptive Behavior.

Question 5: How long did it take you get this result? Because the response to this question is a choice (one month, one quarter, etc.), you may use frequency distributions that describe how data are distributed and that are often presented as lists, ordered by quantity or percentage showing the number of times that each value appears. The following charts shows an example from Business Acumen Training's Impact Evaluation.

For Adoptive Behavior 1, how long did it take you get this result? (n = 125)			
Rank	**Time to Perform**	**Count**	**Percentage**
1	Six months	68	54%
2	One quarter	31	25%
3	One month	20	16%
4	Longer than six months	6	5%

This tells you that the most frequent length to perform Adoptive Behavior 1 was six months.

Question 6: Is this result sustainable? (Will you continue the action that produced this result?) [Yes/No]. A relative comparison is best for this type of data. The BAT result was as shown:

Adoptive Behavior: **obtain and enhance VOC for existing and potential customers.**	
Response (n = 125)	Percentage
Yes	89%
No	11%

What this is telling is that a vast majority of participants feel that the new Adoptive Behavior (VOC) is repeatable and sustainable. You can draw the conclusion that this has a very good chance of becoming a permanent work behavior.

Question 7: Where can these results be validated? Please list company records. This question best lends itself to coded qualitative data. For BAT, some of the codes created from the data were the following:

- Customer penetration strategy presentations
- Product marketing plans
- Customer retention database

Question 8: By what percentage did the use of skills and knowledge from Business Acumen Training contribute to these results? This question lends itself to using measures of central tendency. Continuing with the BAT example, the following chart shows the results.

Response (n = 125)	Value
Mean	81%
Median	80%
Mode	100%
High value	100%
Low value	50%
Range	50
Standard deviation	.15

This tells you that BAT was a significant contributor of the impact being reported.

Question 9 and beyond: These questions deal with the external contribution factors. For each question, you have a Yes/No set of responses (which are best summarized by relative comparisons statistics) and the percentage of contribution for that factor. These data are best represented by measures of central tendency and variability. For BAT, the data were as follows:

Adoptive Behavior: **Did the CRM system contribute to these results?**		
Response (n = 125)	Percentage	Count
Yes	26%	33
No	74%	92

If yes, by what percentage of the result did it contribute?	
Response (n = 33)	Value
Mean	10%
Median	10%
Mode	11%
High value	20%
Low value	2%
Range	48
Standard deviation	.05

These data are telling you that one-fourth (26 percent) of the participants who reported impact feel that the CRM system contributed to the results and that the contribution is approximately 10 percent.

Drawing Conclusions to the Entire Population

For practical reasons you have collected data from a subset of the population called a sample has been studied—as opposed to compiling data about all of the participants. You have collected data via survey for the sample of participants; these data can be subjected to statistical analysis, serving two related purposes, description and inference.

Descriptive statistics summarize the population data by describing what was observed in the sample numerically or graphically. Inferential statistics uses patterns in the sample data to draw inferences about the population represented, accounting for randomness. These inferences may take the form of: answering yes/no questions about the data, estimating numerical characteristics of the data, describing associations within the data, and modeling relationships within the data.

For a sample to be used as a guide to an entire population, it is important that it be truly a representative of that overall population. Representative sampling assured, inferences and conclusions can be safely extended from the sample to the population as a whole. A major problem lies in determining the extent to which the sample chosen is actually representative. Statistics offers methods to estimate and correct for any random trending within the sample and data collection procedures. There are also methods for designing experiments that can lessen these issues at the outset of a study, strengthening its capability to discern truths about the population. Statisticians describe stronger methods as more "robust." If you have concerns about this, seek assistance from a statistician.[2]

Once you are confident that survey data results are representative of the population, you can estimate the entire impact that has been realized. From the Impact Survey, you summarized dollar results with measures of central tendency (mean, median, and mode). If these values are close to each other and the standard deviation is small, follow this procedure for each Adoptive Behavior:

1. Look at your data and answer this question: *What percentage of the sample have successfully adopted?* For example, if 50 percent of the sample has been coded as *Successful Adoption,* you can draw the conclusion that 50 percent of all participants (the population) have successfully adopted. So if 600 participants is the population, 300 would be assumed as *Successful Adoption.*

2. Next answer: *What statistic best describes the results of the sample? Mean, median, or mode?* For example, if you judge that the $5,000 for an Adoptive Behavior is representative, choose that value. You

then can conclude that the mean value applies to the population (all participants).

3. Calculate the total impact for the Adoptive Behavior by multiplying the statistic chosen (in this example, the $5,000 mean) times the *Successful Adoption* participants from the population (in this example, 300). Therefore, the total impact for this Adoptive Behavior is $5,000 × 300 = $1,500,000.

Answering the Impact Questions

You need to answer tentatively two Impact questions and then (validate your initial findings later, with participant interviews and investigating company records). The questions to answer are these:

1. *What impact has the company received from training?* This is relatively easy: sum all the value being reported and discount by the average contribution factor. You may also view it as an average per participant if that is warranted.

2. *How does that impact compare to predicted impact?* Again, this is another easy task: look at what you have found and compare it to the course's Impact Matrix. Are the results ahead, behind, or on track with the predicted impact? Are you seeing unforeseen impact? Are participants doing things related to training and producing impact that was not predicted?

Interpretation is the process of giving meaning to the result of the analysis and deciding the significance and implications of what the data show. Answering the evaluation question means interpreting the analyzed data (quantitative and qualitative) to see if results support or do not support the answers to the evaluation questions.

Step 4: Interview Successful and Unsuccessful Participants

One element of data collection for an Impact Evaluation involves interviews with participants in order to find examples of the best results and to identify those employees who have no or very little impact. You need only interview a subset of the graduates in order to generalize conclusions to the entire population.[3]

From Adoption Evaluation, review the list of participants that you classified as *Unsuccessful Adoption*: this is the list of potential individuals to interview who have no impact. In the Impact Survey results, participants with high-impact results are the group of participants with whom to conduct a successful interview. This is the *High-Impact* pool.

Randomly Select a Sample from Both Groups

You interview enough people in the High-Impact category to find approximately ten best examples of impact. This may involve interviewing fifteen to twenty graduates or more. Note: the more examples found, the stronger is the correlation from this sample to the entire population. However, these numbers are based on the sample size (the number of graduates). With fifty graduates, it is likely that ten to fifteen are in the High-Impact category, which requires a lower number of interviews. The critical factors affecting interviewing are the time and the budget to conduct the interviews. The more interviews that you can conduct the better, but it needs to be within time and budget constraints. For estimation purposes, a single High-Impact interview (conducting the interview and summarizing the result) takes approximately one hour.

Having determined how many High-Impact interviews to conduct, identify which participants to interview. Consider each person in the High-Impact group and choose the people with the most favorable self-reported results.

The next step is to determine how many No Impact interviews to conduct. These interviews are shorter (typically, thirty minutes to interview and summarize results). A determining factor on how many to interview is the size of the No Impact group. If it is relatively small, plan on interviewing everyone. If it is relatively large, start interviewing and continue until you discover the systemic reasons for no impact. Another way of thinking about this is to conduct interviews until you find nothing new.

Inviting the Graduates to the Interview

There are many ways to schedule interview times with participants. The most common method is via e-mail; a sample e-mail for each category of interviewee is given.

High-Impact Interview E-Mail Invitation

From: V.A.L.E. Consulting, LLC

To: Participant Name

Subject: Because you're doing so well with your [course name] skills, we want to know more!

I am an external consultant evaluating the [course name] training for [company name]. You recently completed the [course name] survey—thank you! I have selected you because of your insightful responses and would like to talk further about how you are applying the new skills/knowledge. I would appreciate a thirty-minute phone call with you to understand this more fully.

Please review the following times given and nominate a thirty-minute time slot when I could have this short call with you. Please hit reply, scroll down, complete the right-hand column for each of the three items, and return this e-mail to me. Thank you very much!

The information we discuss will be confidential.

No Impact Interview E-Mail Invitation

From: V.A.L.E. Consulting, LLC

To: Participant Name

Subject: [course name] Follow-Up Survey

You recently completed the [course name] survey. I am an external consultant evaluating this training program for [company name] and am interested in how you applied the new skills/knowledge and would like to have a ten-minute phone call with you to understand this more fully.

Please review the following times given and nominate a ten-minute time slot when I could have this short call with you. Please hit reply, scroll down, complete the right-hand column for each of the three items, and return this e-mail to me. Thank you very much!

The information we discuss will be confidential.

Interview High-Impact Participants

High-Impact interview questions should be focused on such issues as the following:

- Validate what participants have actually done. What actions have they undertaken? How did training contribute toward the results?

- What knowledge and skills from training did they use? What tools/techniques learned in training have they employed? What knowledge or tools did participants have to learn on their own to produce the results?

- What in the environment has enabled or inhibited them as they produced results?

- What are the tangible business results? Gather specific examples. How much of the business result can be directly attributed to training? Are the results sustainable?

- Will they continue to use these new actions and how do they see them being repeated in the future?

Use a semi-structured interview process with probing questions to gather additional data as needed. A semi-structured interview directs the interview conversations. Some of the interview questions may or may not be posed according to the conversation between the evaluator and the participant. The evaluator may pose emerging questions (not listed in the interview protocol) as appropriate according to the interview conversation. Each interview is anticipated to last no more than thirty minutes.

High-Impact Interview Questions (Protocol)

The High-Impact interview uses a set of questions to locate and validate impact data (see Figure 27). The following are a set of standard questions that you may use or modify as you feel necessary.

Demographics. Participant information: note that some of the data are found in the Adoption and Impact survey records. Simply transfer them to the interview sheet for that participant.

- Name [from Impact Survey]
- Data Record Number [from Impact Survey]: this is the row number from the Impact Survey results spreadsheet in which the participant's impact data are stored. You use this during interview preparation to review the participant's results.
- Adoptive Behavior Number [from Impact Survey]: at times, participants will have reported on more than one Adoptive Behavior during the Impact Survey. This element on the protocol indicates which behavior and its subsequent results are being interviewed.
- Date: date of the interview
- Participant position: the role the participant currently fulfills in the company
- Location: city/area where the participants works
- Time with the company: length of service with the company

Supervisor support. It is useful to gather data on the involvement and support of the interviewee's supervisor. These two questions provide these data. Use probing questions to gather further data as needed. Note: most likely, you will move back and forth between questions until you have all the data you need.

- Did you meet with your supervisor prior to training? If so, what was discussed?
- Did you meet with your supervisor afterward? If so, what was discussed? [Probe regarding level of support.]

Impact. This is the heart of the interview, and this discussion is held for each Adoptive Behavior. Take careful notes about what participants did. Record the outcome(s), and always ask for a metric. For example, if the participants says, "we increased productivity," probe with "What was the result?" or "Estimate the increase in productivity." The questions to ask in this section of the interview are as follows:

- Tell me about your goal and how you have put it into practice. I'm interested in the outcomes from what you've been doing. Is this sustainable? [Watch for the metric.] Specifically, review these items (from the Impact Survey):
  - Action taken
  - Outcome(s) [Give an example and the implications or results from doing this.]

- Do you have another example? At times, employees have additional Impact data beyond their original goal—in other words, they are using the skills and seeing impact in other areas. You may find a gem of impact here. If so, repeat the *Action Taken* and *Outcome(s)* questions to gather as much data as possible, including any metrics.

- I'm interested in knowing how else the program has benefited you and/or the company.

- What would you say was the greatest impact for you from the training? What difference has it made to you at work? These are personal value statements and typically reinforce the impact found in the earlier portion of the interview.

No Impact Interview Questions (Protocol)

Participants with no impact are those who in the Adoption Evaluation were classified as *Unsuccessful Adoption*. The purpose of the No Impact interview is to talk to enough employees in order to determine whether there are any systemic elements that have kept them from adopting their goals and therefore having no impact. These interviews are usually short, approximately ten minutes, with twenty minutes to summarize (see Figure 28).

Demographics. Participant information: note that some of the data are found in the Adoption and Impact survey records. Simply transfer them to the interview sheet for that participant.

- First name [from Adoption Survey]
- Last name [from Adoption Survey]

- Data record number [from Adoption Survey]: this is the row number from the Adoption Survey results spreadsheet in which the participant's adoption data are stored. You use this during interview preparation to review the participant's results.

- Date: date of the interview

- Participant position: the role the participant currently fulfills in the company

- Location: city/area where the participants works

- Time with the company: length of service with the company

Supervisor support. As with the High-Impact interview, capture data on supervisor support to see if it is part of the reason for No Impact. Questions used here are as follows:

- Did you meet with your supervisor prior to training? If so, what was discussed?

- Did you meet with your supervisor afterward? If so, what was discussed? [Probe regarding level of support.]

Reasons for Unsuccessful Adoption. You want to discover, via the participants' own words, why they have made no progress. Note: ask questions in a non-judgmental manner so as not to "shut down" or offend the participant. Use probing questions as needed to gather further data. The question used here is this: "*You said on the survey that you had made no progress on your goal/s. Tell me about your goal/s and why you've made no progress.*"

Undisclosed Impact. Other benefits the course has provided may be present. At times, value statements emerge in these interviews when you probe in this area. Use this question:

- Has the program benefited you in any way?

Finally, close the questioning with the following:

- Any other comments?

Conducting an Effective Interview

Here are some tips for conducting an effective High-Impact or No Impact interview.

- **Listen effectively.** Be a good listener; know how to redirect a conversation to get the critical information as quickly as possible. Listen without judging.

Name: _____   Data Record Number: _____   Adoptive Behavior Number: _____

Interview Date: _____   Participant Location: _____

Participant Position: _____   Participant Time with Company: _____

Q1. Did you meet with your supervisor prior to training? If so, what was discussed?

Q2. Did you meet with your supervisor afterward? If so, what was discussed? [Probe regarding level of support]

Q3. Tell me about your goal and how you have put it into practice. I'm interested in the outcomes from what you've been doing. [Is this sustainable?] [Watch for the metric]

ACTION TAKEN:

OUTCOMES:

Q4. Do you have another example?

Q5. I'm interested in knowing how else the program has benefited you, the company, or both.

Q6. What would you say was the greatest impact for you from the training? What difference has it made to you at work?

Figure 27: High-Impact Interview Form

Name: _____ Data Record Number: _____ Adoptive Behavior Number: _____

Interview Date: _____ Participant Location: _____

Participant Position: _____ Participant Time with Company: _____

Q1. Did you meet with your supervisor prior to training? If so, what was discussed?

Q2. Did you meet with your supervisor afterward? If so, what was discussed? [Probe regarding level of support]

Q3. You said on the survey that you had made no progress on your goal/s. Tell me about your goal/s and why you've made no progress.

Q4. Has the program benefited you in any way?

Q5. Any other comments?

Figure 28: No Impact Interview Form

- **Prepare.** Review the employee's Adoption and Impact Survey data prior to the interview.

- **Ease on in.** Start with easy to respond to questions—just follow the interview protocol.

- **Set the tone.** Let the interviewee know how the data will be used and that everything said will be held in strictest confidence. A standard phrase is this: *"Mary, I am an external consultant who has been hired by the company to evaluate the effectiveness of the XYZ Training Course. You have been selected from the people who completed the course survey last week. I am interested in how you have applied what you learned in class and what impact it has had on you, your team, or the company. What you tell me will be held in strictest confidence. I may, however, include your story in a summary report without your name. Are you okay to proceed?"*

  Also, express your appreciation for the time that participants have taken to talk to you. Explain how the interview will proceed and then try to follow that format as closely as possible.

- **Use the script.** Follow the interview protocol.

- **Listen to your instincts.** As you hear things regarding Adoption and Impact, continue to probe until you feel you have uncovered everything.

- **Know what you want.** If you've set aside thirty minutes for the interview, do your best to stick with that schedule. But be prepared to cut the interview short and jump to the concluding questions. Don't waste your time or the interviewee's if you are not talking about Impact data. The most common things that interviewees bring up that sidetrack you are discussing how well they liked the class, complaining about the company in general, etc.

- **Write it down.** Forget about remembering everything that transpires during an interview. You'll want to take notes so that you can review at a later time. This is especially important if you're interviewing many people.

- **Probe.** As you uncover areas that you feel are promising, investigate further by asking probing questions. Some common probing questions are as follows:
  - Tell me more about that.
  - When you did that, what was the result?

- How did you do that?
- What did you do specifically? What was the result?
- You mentioned [insert his/her result]; can you place a metric on that result? What is the metric?
- What did you find to be the most challenging thing when you did that?
- Will you continue to do this? Why?
- What other things have happened as a result of doing this?

- **Test for understanding.** Paraphrase back to interviewees what you have heard. They will either confirm that you understand or add further information.

- **End with a thank-you.** Thank the interviewees and remind them how their data will be used.

Documenting the Interview

Take copious notes during the interview, and document the interview immediately after you hang up the phone or conclude the meeting—don't wait for a few days or even a few hours. You will forget items quickly. A good rule of thumb is to allow the same amount of time to record as you spend interviewing. In other words, if you plan to conduct a High-Impact interview for thirty minutes, schedule the thirty minutes immediately following it to record the interview.

For each interview, create a word processing file to store the results. If you conduct fifteen interviews, you should have fifteen files on your computer. These files are your completed data collection instruments and are used when you analyze the results to find the Impact profiles.

Create Impact Profiles

Print the interview summaries for your review. Read each one, and sort them into two piles (the ones that are the best examples of Impact as aligned with the Impact Matrix and those that are not as powerful). Use the following items as criteria for placing an interview summary in the Impact Profile pile:

- Direct impact on and value to the business can be traced to training via the participant's Intention Goals and Adoptive Behavior.

- Adoption of training has made a measurable difference.

- Results validated in the interview support the data from the Impact Survey.

- Results are in alignment with the predicted Impact identified in the Impact Matrix.

The interviews that pass the preceding test become your *Impact Profiles*—examples of the best results that the training has produced. These validate the Impact data reported in the Impact Survey and are further proof of Impact created. The Impact Profile is a one-page synopsis of the participant's story. Review these profiles, and answer these questions: *Do the profiles support the answers to the questions you determined from the Impact Survey data analysis?* Those questions are the following:

1. What impact has the company received from training?

2. How does that impact compare to predicted impact?

Now you document each profile. First, sanitize the Impact Profiles by removing anything that identifies the participant. A typical Impact Profile has the following elements:

- **Headline:** should tell the reader what was done and the impact that was realized. Examples of Impact Profile headlines are as follows:
  - Process redesign reduces cycle time by 15 percent while decreasing customer complaints by 95 percent and saves $150K in first six months.
  - Scanning system saves time and cost—savings of sixty-five minutes for each document processed—$15K annual cost savings.
  - Web-based data management system saves $250K per year, increased customer satisfaction, and improved employee morale.

- **The impact story:** one or two paragraphs that state what the participant did. See Figure 29 for an example.

- **Outcomes:** the impact to the company. In some cases, the impact is quantifiable; in others, the results are "softer" but nevertheless acceptable. See Figure 29 for an example.

Step 5: Collect Impact Data from Company Records

You should now have a clear picture as to the impact that the training is providing and whether or not it is as predicted. An issue that exists with the current impact data is that it is self-reported via the Impact Survey and somewhat validated with the Impact Interviews. This is good and, many times, sufficient for you to produce the Impact Dashboard and draw your conclusions on the value of training. If you choose, you can further build your case by collecting

---

Profile #1 : Open-ended and probing questions led to out-of-the box thinking, resulting in significant time savings

Q. What did you do?
We needed material for an upcoming project and the crew informed me that they needed to go to an out-of-service area, tear out the material, and use it, since no material was available. I used open-ended questions to get them to think out of the box about other places where the material could be. I then used probing questions to get them to even think deeper.

What happened?
As we were talking, one guy said, "I think there may be some material at this spot." Then that triggered another guy to think of an additional location for material.

So what happened?
They went out on the way to the next day's job site and got all the material we needed and did not have to go to the out-of-service area.

Outcome
Q. What was the result?
Two things: (1) the total time to get the material was 1 man-hour; if we had gone and removed the materials from the out-of-service area it would have been 32 man-hours; furthermore, (2) because we did not have to remove material we avoided all those potential safety hazards.

How much money was saved due to this time savings?
We saved at least $2,000.

Figure 29: Impact Profile Example

data from existing company records. This type of data is known as *extant data*. Extant data are existing data, information, and observations that have been collected or that are available for use in the assessment and evaluation processes.[4] Basically, you analyze records and files that the company already has, rather than set out to gather additional information. Where and what files you look at depend on the impact being claimed by participants (e.g., sales figures, attendance figures, call-backs for repair, etc.). Customer e-mails, tech support log files, marketing and business plans, business requirements, documents, and vision statements are just a few of the types of information that help you validate the impact.

The quickest way to gather extant data is to ask High-Impact interview participants to provide the documentation that proves their case (assuming that they have permission to share it with you). This typically comes in the form of presentations, spreadsheets, sales records, financial statements, manufacturing reports, time and motion studies, etc. When you receive the documentation, review it and ensure that you have sufficient information to validate claimed impact.

At times, the participant no longer has the backup documentation or it simply does not exist. This does not mean that you do not include the impact in your Impact Dashboard, but you may need to add a disclaimer to the report stating so.

Step 6: Create Impact Dashboard and Evaluation Report

For Impact, two reporting methods are used:

1. An Impact Dashboard that summarizes the Impact found
2. A formal Impact Evaluation Report that provides impact findings, impact profiles, recommendations, program description, and details on the evaluation methodology

A typical Impact Dashboard is made up of four pages/sections: (1) payback, results, and key findings; (2) impact by Adoptive Behavior; (3) impact examples and recommendations; and (4) the Impact Profiles. Let's look at each section using data from our Business Acumen Training example. Note: for this example, BAT has been delivered for three years. An Impact Dashboard was created for years one and two, but they are not being shown here.

Impact Dashboard, Page 1 (see Figure 30)

This is the summary page, which contains three sections. Section 1 is the training's Payback Chart. It is a line graph of the costs over the years, plotted along with the impact realized. In corporate finance, the payback period is a simple measure of the time it takes to recover capital spent on an investment. In this case, it is the period for impact results to recover the training costs. For BAT, payback period was eighteen months.

Section 2 is a table showing predicted versus actual training costs and impact for the three years. A three-year ROI is also shown. In this example, BAT produced good value to the company, but it was below predications.

Section 3 is the Key Findings, where you document for the reader the main findings from the Impact Evaluation.

Impact Dashboard, Page 2 (see Figure 31)

The second page is detailed impact by Adoptive Behavior and is shown as a table of results. In the first column, list the Adoptive Behavior being reported. The next section is a series of data regarding adoption results and contains the number of people predicted to adopt and the actual number who did adopt. An *Adoption Ratio* is calculated from these data by dividing the number who actually adopted by the predicted number; the result is shown as a percentage. Any value greater than 100 percent is meeting the Adoption Success Gate (shown in the final column in this section). The final section is a series of columns that show impact results by Adoptive Behavior. The first two columns show predicted impact (from the Impact Matrix) and actual impact. Note: actual impact is the summary data from the Impact Survey results. The *Impact Ratio* is calculated as dividing actual impact by predicted impact; the result is shown as a percentage. Again, any Impact Ratio greater than 100 percent has met the Impact Success Gate.

Impact Dashboard, Page 3 (see Figure 32)

The third page has two sections. The first section contains Impact Examples, which are the headlines of the Impact Profiles starting on page four of the Dashboard. The second section includes any recommendations you wish to make that may increase impact.

Impact Dashboard, Page 4 (see Figure 33)

Page four and beyond, if necessary, provide a listing of the Impact Profiles that you created from the Impact Interviews. These are the best examples of impact and provide the reader with evidence (beyond the numbers) of the impact provided by training.

Write the Formal Impact Evaluation Report

A formal Impact Evaluation Report is written in conjunction with the Impact Dashboard. The purpose of the report is to provide the Steering Committee and any other interested parties with a complete picture of the impact that training has provided to the business. The outline for the report typically is as follows:

- Introduction: brief description of the program and the associated evaluation efforts. This section typically contains these items:
  - Course name
  - Evaluator names(s)
  - Purpose of the evaluation

Impact Dashboard Page 1

Business Acumen Training Payback

	2008	2009	2010
Cumulative Cost	$200	$484	$705
Cumulative Impact	$125	$495	$1,250

Business Acumen Training Results (3 years)

	Predicted			Actual		
	Part.	Cost	Impact	Part.	Cost	Impact
2008	100	$250	$242	75	$200	$125
2009	100	$205	$485	135	$284	$370
2010	100	$205	$727	105	$221	$755
Total	300	$660	$1,454	315	$705	$1,250
		ROI	220%		ROI	177%

Key Findings:

- 3 years of Business Acumen Training has produced a return of $545K to the company ($1,250K impact; $705K cost). This is 69% of predicted return.
- Training costs for 3 years were 7% above predicted costs.
- 3-year ROI was 177% actual versus an predicted ROI of 220%. Still very good, but below expectations.
- Training payback was 18 months.
- Voice of Customer (VOC) and Product/Services Roadmaps were the most commonly used skills producing the most impact.

Figure 30: Impact Dashboard, Page 1

Impact Dashboard Page 2

Course Title: Business Acumen Training
Training Dates: 2008–2010

Number of Participants: 315

Adoptive Behavior	No. Who Adopt			Adoption	Impact for the Year (K)			Impact
	Predicted	Actual	Adoption Ratio	Successful	Predicted	Actual	Impact Ratio	Met?
Obtain and enhance VOC for existing and potential customers.	45	68	151%	Y	$338	$356	105%	Y
Develop products/services roadmaps aligned with the goals of the customer while maximizing recurring revenue opportunity.	75	110	147%	Y	$720	$670	93%	N
Facilitate sessions with their team, discussing with them the ways in which they help to improve key financial metrics.	30	6	20%	N	$338	$221	65%	N
Lay out planned activities and corresponding monetary resources for the fiscal year, including recurring annual expenses and non-recurring investments in special projects.	12	1	8%	N	$58	$4	7%	N
Total	**162**	**185**	**114%**	**Y**	**$1,454**	**$1,250**	**86%**	**N**

Figure 31: Impact Dashboard, Page 2

Impact Dashboard Page 3

Impact Examples

- Sales increased by $2.5K by using Voice of Customer

- Break-even Analysis results in $175K of additional Operating Profit

- Managing Inventory, Costs and Cash Flow save $42K annually

- Manager Changes Order Entry Process, Customer Satisfaction increased by 32%

- Total Asset Turnover ratio increased from 1.78 to 2.10

Recommendations

- Executives reinforce participants to lay out planned activities and corresponding monetary resources for the fiscal year because this behavior has little adoption and impact

- Supervisors be encouraged meet with the attendees (singly or in a group) after BAT and ask about their goals and if the supervisor can help in any way

Figure 32: Impact Dashboard, Page 3

Impact Dashboard Page 4

Impact Profiles

Profiles # 1: Sales Increased by $2.5K by using Voice of Customer

Q. What did you do?

For the Walnut Locking residential series, I identified a hierarchical set of "customer needs" where each need had an assigned priority which indicated its importance to the customer. My first use of the VOC was in positioning. By understanding the dimensions of competition, we were able to indentify how to differentiate our brand to achieve a 0.5% growth in sales. One of those needs was electronic keypad Entry Locks and Deadbolts with no keys to hide, lose, carry, or forget. That feature was introduced to the marketplace in Q1 for this line of products.

Outcome

Q. What was the result?

Following product launch, we saw a 0.7% increase in sales for the Walnut line. The increase in sales so far has produced additional sales of $2,500.

Profile #2: Break-even Analysis Results in $175K of Additional Operating Profit

Q. What did you do?

I reviewed business operations and determined we use low operating leverage. I also determined the break-even level for each of the various products and services that we sell. We then changed our pricing and spending decisions accordingly.

Outcome

Q. What was the result?

We passed the break-even point and increased our Operating Profit (OP) by 0.5%. This has resulted in $175K of additional OP last year.

Figure 33: Impact Dashboard, Page 4

- How the report is organized: (a) Background and Methodology, (b) Key Findings, (c) Recommendations, (d) Impact Survey Results (Appendix A), (e) Impact Profiles (Appendix B)

- Training Background and Methodology: course title, business purpose, and delivery history (target audience, when, where, by whom)

- Evaluation Methodology: describes the Impact methodology

- Key Findings: you document what your analysis of the impact interviews has told you. You may have as many key findings as you deem necessary. Make sure that you reference the Impact Dashboard data as needed.

- Recommendations: you suggest actions that the business might consider to sustain and/or improve impact.

- Appendix A: Detailed Impact Survey Results: the data from the Impact Dashboard are restated. This is done because some readers of the report may not have seen the Adoption data and need to understand them to comprehend the Impact data.

- Appendix B: Impact Profiles: these are examples of the best adoption and impact cases so that the reader has an understanding of what is actually happening in the field as a result of the training.

Summary

An Impact Evaluation addresses the following questions: *What business results can be traced to the goal adoption of participants? Are results as predicted to the business? What is the typical profile of a participant who has achieved results? What additional business results (value) could be achieved if graduates who have little/no adoption were to adopt their goals?*

The reason to train should be to improve the company's bottom line. By measuring the effect on the company profits from participant intentions, adoption, and impact and comparing that with the predicted value, a company can determine its return on investment and can maximize organizational and business results.

Chapter 6

How to Get Started— Implementing Predictive Evaluation

So you've decided that you're going to do a PE, and, yikes, it is your first one! First, answer these questions:

- Will PE be used in deciding whether or not to move forward with training?

- Why is the evaluation being done; that is, what decisions does the company want to make during the evaluation?

- Who are the key stakeholders who should receive evaluation reports? What do they want from the evaluation?

- What elements of a PE will provide the data to aid in the decisions that you and/or stakeholders want to make?

- When is the information needed?

- What resources are available to conduct the evaluation? Can a Steering Committee be formed to aid with the evaluation? Will internal resources be used or will you employ external evaluation resources?

- Is funding available? What projects will be delayed or not done if PE is implemented?

- What existing evaluation practices are in place? Can they be leveraged and used in the PE? Will PE replace some of these practices?

The answers to the questions attempt to get at the purpose of the evaluation and what is prompting it. Implementing your first Predictive Evaluation can be a bit intimidating, but, as with any effort, it gets easier and quicker as you do it. If you would like to ease into PE efforts, start with Intentions Evaluation and then move to an Adoption effort; finally, try an Impact Evaluation. No matter what evaluation element you pick, make sure that you always start with Predicting.

Next, you need a plan of action—the **PE Plan**. The key to a successful PE is in the planning. Often, evaluation planning is ignored in favor of getting on with the work. However, many people fail to realize the value of an evaluation plan in saving time and money and preventing problems.

Planning Step 1: Questions PE Answers

A PE is successful when the needs of the stakeholders have been met. A stakeholder is anybody directly or indirectly impacted by the evaluation. As a first step, it is important to identify the stakeholders for your PE. It is not always easy to identify the stakeholders of an evaluation, particularly those impacted indirectly. Examples of stakeholders are as follows:

- The Head of the Training and Development organization
- Key executives from various business units or staff functions. Note: these may be represented by a Steering Committee or other such body.
- Instructional designers, course developers, and instructors (internal or external)
- External training suppliers (to a lesser extent)

Once you understand who the stakeholders are, the next step is to establish their needs. The best way to do this is by conducting stakeholder interviews. The questions that you ask stakeholders can depend on (1) who you are talking to and (2) how they fit into the overall picture. When formulating stakeholder questions, ask yourself the following:

- What do you want to find out?
- How many people can you interview?
- What will you do with the data to help guide the PE?
- What is the underlying reason for asking a specific question?

Some questions that you may wish to use with the stakeholders are as follows:

- What business issue(s) is this training going to help in solving?
- Why does this issue exist?
- Why do you want an evaluation?
- What kind of information would you like to see from the evaluation?
- What decisions will you make based on this evaluation information?
- What is your timetable for getting evaluation information? How would you like to see it and receive it?
- Who else should I talk to?

Take time during the interviews to draw out the true needs that create real benefits. Often stakeholders talk about needs that aren't relevant and don't deliver benefits. These can be recorded and set as a low priority.

The next step—once you have conducted all the stakeholder interviews and have a comprehensive list of needs—is to prioritize them. From the prioritized list, create a set of questions the evaluation will answer (see the following example).

Elements in an Evaluation Plan

In addition to the evaluation questions, other elements of the evaluation plan arise from stakeholder interviews and your research into the course. Each element that you should consider as part of the plan is shown in the following table.

Element	Description
Course to be evaluated	List the title and purpose for the course. Provide a history (business reason) for the course and what it is intended to achieve. For new courses (ones yet to be developed), these data can be found in the needs analysis and/or instructional design documents. For existing courses, use the current training materials.
Purpose of the evaluation	Documents why the PE is being undertaken and how the information will be used (comes from stakeholder requirements). Example: *Our approach is based on moving away from the typical measurement of activity or level-based measures in favor of focusing on value-driven continuous improvement efforts. This ensures that the training investment creates value and produces the behaviors and results that lead to the desired business outcomes.*
Questions the evaluation will answer	These are the basic building blocks for the PE and help determine the elements (Intention, Adoption, and Impact) of this evaluation. They are the questions that key stakeholders would like to see answered. Examples: **Are participant intentions and beliefs upon program completion aligned with desired values?** The intentions evaluation captures goals and beliefs, compares them against the agreed-on standard for goals and list of beliefs, and creates a monthly dashboard that shows the degree to *(Continued...)*

Element	Description
	which goals are focused and attainable. Evaluating intentions allows early identification of problems or factors that negatively impact adoption and impact.
	Are participants using (adopting) the skills on the job? This is adoption evaluation; it assesses how much of the training has been tried on-the-job and successfully integrated into the participant's work behavior. Evaluating adoption at more than one checkpoint during the year allows us to pinpoint the extent of adoption and identify recommendations to increase it.
	Is the training program contributing to achievement of the business outcomes? If yes, to what degree? If no, why not? Although some outcomes take longer than others to emerge, there should be some evidence after six months that participant's changed attitudes and behaviors are having a positive effect in relation to the stated business outcomes.
Key Stakeholders	These are the individuals who have a vested interest in the evaluation information.

Once this is completed, it's time to move on and look at the evaluation deliverables.

Planning Step 2: Evaluation Deliverables

Using the evaluation questions and other planning elements you have defined in Step 1, create a list of information that the PE needs to deliver in order to answer the evaluation questions. Specify when and how each item must be delivered. These are the elements of the PE (Predicting Training's Value, Intention Evaluation, Adoption Evaluation, and/or Impact Evaluation).

Add the deliverables to the evaluation plan, with an estimated delivery date. More accurate delivery dates can be established during the scheduling phase, which is next.

Planning Step 3: Evaluation Schedule

Create a list of tasks that need to be carried out for each deliverable identified in Step 2. For each task, identify the following:

- The amount of effort (hours or days) required to complete the task
- The resource that will carry out the task

Scheduling an evaluation is a factor of size, scope, volume, type of course, the number of participants, and which elements of a PE are being performed. To help in estimating time, use the following table.

Evaluation Element	Task	Hours (est.)
Planning	Researching course to be evaluated	4–8 hours
	Interviewing stakeholders	4–8 hours
	Writing Evaluation Plan	2–4 hours
	Securing approval to proceed	1–2 hours
Predicting Training's Value	Securing Steering Committee members	2–4 hours
	Facilitating Steering Committee to build the Impact Matrix	8 hours
	Documenting the Impact Matrix	2 hours
	Validating the Impact Matrix	4–8 hours
	Reviewing validation data with Steering Committee and finalizing the Impact Matrix	8 hours
	Working with Steering Committee secure to present Impact Matrix and approval to move forward	10–12 hours
Intention Evaluation	Intention: developing goal sheet	2–4 hours
	Training instructors on goal sheet administration	1 hour
	Entering Intention Goals into database/ spreadsheet	2–3 minutes per goal sheet
	Formatting database and data cleansing	2 hours per analysis. For example, if you judge goals monthly, schedule 2 hours per month.
	Judging goals	1 minute per goal
	Preparing Intention Evaluation statistics, charts, and graphs	2 hours per analysis
	Produce Intention Dashboard	1–2 hours
Adoption Evaluation	Developing and testing the Adoption Survey	4 hours
	Survey administration (data collection)	2 hours
	Data cleansing and statistic creation	2–4 hours

(Continued...)

Evaluation Element	Task	Hours (est.)
	Judging adoption	2–4 hours, depending on the number of respondents
	Data analysis and drawing conclusions— coding participants as *Successfully Adopted* or *Unsuccessful Adopted*	2 hours
	Produce Adoption Dashboard	1–2 hours
	Presenting findings to Steering Committee	2 hours
Impact Evaluation	Developing and testing the Impact Survey	4 hours
	Survey administration (data collection)	2 hours
	Data cleansing and statistic creation	2–4 hours
	Scheduling Interviews (High-Impact and No Impact participants)	1 hour
	Conduct and transcribe High-Impact interviews	1 hour per interview
	Conduct and transcribe No Impact interviews	30 minutes per interview
	Data analysis	2–4 hours
	Produce Impact Dashboard	1–2 hours
	Produce Formal Evaluation Report	2–4 hours
	Presenting findings to Steering Committee	2 hours

Once you have established the amount of effort for each task, you can work out the effort required for each deliverable and determine an accurate delivery date. Update your deliverables section with the more accurate delivery dates.

A common problem discovered at this point occurs when an evaluation has an imposed delivery deadline from the sponsor or Steering Committee that is not realistic based on your estimates. If you discover that this is the case, you must contact the Committee members immediately. The options you have in this situation are the following:

- Renegotiate the due dates.
- Employ additional resources.
- Reduce the scope of the evaluation.

Use the evaluation schedule to justify pursuing one of these options.

Congratulations! Having followed all the preceding steps, you should have a good PE plan. Remember to update your plan as the evaluation progresses and measure progress against the plan.

Performing the PE

With the project plan in place and approval to proceed, implement the PE using the PE sequence.

1. Choose the course you wish to evaluate; it can be a new course design or a course that already exists. Note: this should have been done when you developed the PE plan.

2. Review the course to understand fully what it is, what it is supposed to teach, how participants learn the material, what business issues it addresses, who is to attend, how they attend, what pre-course preparations are in place, what post-course support mechanisms exist, who are the sponsors, what sponsors see as the purpose for the course.

3. Form a committee to predict training value; create the Impact Matrix and present the predictions to key decision makers *(see Chapter 2: Predicting Training's Value)*.

4. Evaluate Intentions: during course pilot and for every session thereafter *(see Chapter 3: Intention Evaluation)*. Improve results as necessary by conducting root cause analysis and implementing corrective action.

5. Evaluate Adoption: determine how often and when to conduct Adoption Evaluations *(see Chapter 4: Adoption Evaluation)*. Improve results as necessary by conducting root cause analysis and implementing corrective action.

6. Evaluate Impact: determine how often and when to conduct Impact Evaluations *(see Chapter 5: Impact Evaluation)*. Improve results as necessary by conducting root cause analysis and implementing corrective action.

PE and Continuous Improvement

One aspect of PE is to seek small improvements in course design, delivery, and transfer with the objective of increasing impact. Continuous improvement is one of the tools that underpins the philosophies of PE. Through constant study and revision of Intention, Adoption, and Impact, better training occurs, resulting in increased impact. Continuous Improvement is a set of activities designed to bring gradual but continual improvement to training results through constant review.

The principles that underlie Continuous Improvement using PE are the following:

Focus on the stakeholder. Training is designed, developed, and delivered to meet stakeholder requirements and needs. To accomplish this, stakeholders were solicited in the planning phase and their requirements were built into the PE predictions. A decision is then made by stakeholders as to proceed with training, based on the attractiveness of benefits (value) to be gained. Intention, Adoption, and Impact results are then measured from the perspective of the stakeholder.

A preventive approach. "Do it right the first time" instead of correcting through evaluation (inspection) if possible. This requires a systematic instructional design process (such as ADDIE [Analysis Design Development Implementation Evaluation]) to ensure that the training will deliver the Intention, Adoption, and Impact results that stakeholders require.

Management by data. Fact rather than supposition drives continuous improvement actions. PE data—communicated in the Dashboards against respective Success Gates—direct decision in improvements and outcomes.

Commit to ongoing improvement. Each time that Success Gates are reached, consider setting new and improved Intention, Adoption, or Impact success measures. PE is not a project or a task with a definite end point, but an ongoing commitment to seek out opportunities to deliver better results.

Cross-functional problem solving. Training problems do not usually fall neatly into a single function such as design, development, delivery, management support, etc. They usually call for solutions that cut horizontally across organizational functions. People with different responsibilities and talents need to develop habits of working together to improve training and its results.

Constancy of leadership commitment. A commitment to PE continuous improvement must be a way of life, built into the fabric of the company. In most organizations, this represents a fundamental change in culture and values. Tenacious and visible commitment of top leadership to PE is required if employees inside and outside of the training function are to be motivated to make the investment to change.

	Rating
1 = Not at all 2 = To a small extent 3 = Somewhat 4 = To a large extent 5 = To a very great extent	
Design	
Instructional design and course development folllows a similar process used by the enterprise for design/development of business products	
Instructional design and course development have quality review gates built in at each stage to ensure consistent application and quality	
Instructional design uses an Impact Matrix to connect design to business results	
Support	
Participants and their managers meet prior to training to create a personal learning map that predicts application of learning to individual and department results	
Participants create a personal action plan during training to plan on-the-job application to achieve personal and department goals	
Post-training participant goals are formalized and added to participant's annual objetives/development efforts	
Managers provide continuous coaching and support as participants apply new skills and knowledge	
Evaluation	
Intention goals and beliefs are predicted and documented in an Impact Matrix	
Adoptive Behaviors are predicted and documented in an Impact Matrix	
Business results and impact are predicted and documented in an Impact Matrix	
Intention goals and beliefs are judged and an Intention score is measured against a success gate	
Adoption results are captured and are measured against a success gate	
Impact results are captured and are measured against a success gate	
Training's value creation results are reported regularly to sponsoring organizations	
The Training and development function reports its organizational merit and worth via a scorecard methodology	
Total (sum of scores)	

Figure 34: PE Organizational Assessment

PE Organizational Assessment

Is your company ready to realize the maximum benefits that PE provides? What organizational, procedural, and cultural elements need changing with respect to PE? The Predictive Evaluation Organizational Assessment (PEOA) analyzes the company's environment and readiness to adopt and support an enterprise-wide PE approach. The Learning Function is assessed on fifteen dimensions, which are critical if PE is to be successfully integrated into the organization. The PEOA is shown in Figure 34.

Instructions: Read the statement and indicate your agreement using the following scale:

1. Not at all

2. To a small extent

3. Somewhat

4. To a large extent

5. To a very great extent

Sum the scores to arrive at your results.

If your results are ...	Then you are ...	and the Training and Development function is ...
75–68	Optimized	creating value for the enterprise, operating at world-class levels, and benchmarked as best-in-class.
67–60	Established	creating value for the enterprise.
59–52	Responsive	at times creating value for the enterprise.
51–15	Aware	aware of the elements to create value.

Summary

Because of the nature of PE, you cannot start with Adoption or Impact. The sequence is (1) Predict, (2) Intention, (3) Adoption, and (4) Impact. With some courses, you may stop at Intention only. In other courses, you may perform Intention and Adoption only. In others yet, you may perform a full PE. The choice is up to you and the needs of your company.

Glossary

Action Plan A set of clearly written statements describing in measurable terms the specific actions that the participant intends to apply on-the-job as a result of the training.

Adoption The results of participants applying new skills as part of their work behavior (routine).

Adoption Rate Percentage of participants who have reported successful adoption.

Adoption Success Rate The percentage of participants who have successfully implemented. their Intention Goals. This is a measure of transference from training to the workplace.

Analysis A method of studying the nature of training and determining its essential features and its relations with respect to Intention, Adoption, and Impact.

Belief A conviction, idea, or faith that a participant forms from attending a training program.

Confidence interval The interval bounded by confidence limits. This is the plus-or-minus figure; this type of data is often reported in newspaper or television opinion poll results.

Confidence level This is expressed as a percentage and represents how often the true percentage of the population that would pick an answer lies within the confidence interval. A 95 percent confidence level means that you can be 95 percent certain that the conclusions you draw are real; the 99 percent confidence level means that you can be 99 percent certain.

Dashboard A report that monitors key results from training. Dashboards may be created for Intention, Adoption, and Impact Evaluations.

Data Collection Return Rate A minimum amount of returns from Adoption and Impact surveys, so that the conclusions drawn are realistic and represent what is actually happening.

Evaluate To judge or determine the significance, worth, or quality of a training program.

Evaluation	The process of determining significance or worth, usually by careful appraisal and study. It includes the analysis and comparison of actual progress vs. prior plans, oriented toward improving plans for future implementation.
Force Field Analysis	Tool to depict visually the forces and their effects on training Impact.
Formal Impact	Provides impact findings, success profiles, recommendations, program.
Evaluation Report	description, and details on the evaluation methodology.
External Contribution Factor	Amount to reduce predicted and actual Impact as a result of external and internal factors.
Goal	The result or achievement toward which the participant's effort is directed after training; aim; end.
Goal Analysis Spreadsheet	A worksheet that is arranged in the manner of a mathematical matrix and contains a multicolumn analysis of participant goals for easy reference on a single sheet.
Goal Distribution (Intention Dashboard)	Shows how the participants' goals are distributed across the course modules.
Goal Planning Worksheet	See Action Plan.
Goals Submitted (Intention Dashboard)	The percentage of participants who submitted goals.
High Impact	Participants who have successfully adopted and reported positive impact on the business.
Impact	Adopted behaviors practiced over time (repetition), producing results on the business.
Impact Categories	During Adoption evaluation, participants' self-reported impact usually falls into one of three categories: High Impact, Low Impact, or No Impact.
Impact Dashboard	Summarizes the Impact in a dashboard format.
Impact Evaluation	Assesses the changes to organizational results that can be attributed to the use of new skills mastered in training.

Impact Matrix	A rectangular array of training goals, beliefs, adoption examples, impact results, and a reduction factor that, when combined using certain rules, predict the Impact from training.
Impact Profile	The specific instances that tell the best success stories of a few graduates and their impact to the business.
Intention	Participants' plans to use what they have learned; written in the form of goal statements.
Intention Score	Percentage of learner goals and beliefs that have been judged acceptable to the total goal and beliefs written.
Interview	A formal meeting in which one or more persons (evaluator) question, consult, or evaluate graduates on their Adoption and possible Impact results.
Knowledge	Information, data, or facts provided to participants via training.
Low Impact	Participants who have tried or will try the new skills but are unlikely to have a positive impact on the business.
No Impact	Participants who have tried and given up or have not tried the new skills and who will not create a positive impact on the business.
On-the-job Actions	The on-the-job observable tasks that participants perform as a result of training.
Participant	An employee who attends a training program.
Population	In an Adoption Evaluation, the employees who have graduated from the training program.
Practice	Habitual or customary performance; operation of skills learned in a training program.
Prediction	A statement or claim that a particular event will occur in the future in more certain terms than a forecast.
Predictive Evaluation	Determining training's success in three areas: Intention, Adoption, and Impact. Collecting data to assess if predictions have been met (the Success Gates) and implementing continuous improvement actions when results are below the predictions.
Rate of Adoption	The percentage of participants who have successfully integrated their goals into their everyday work routine.
Sample size	The portion of the population to be surveyed in an Adoption evaluation.

Skill	Ability, talent, expertise, performance, or competence provided to the participant via training.
SOS + D Model	Format for Intention Goal composition made up of (1) Specific: The goal is free of ambiguity, and it is clear what participants will be doing, (2) Observable: Others will be able to see participants doing this, (3) Significant: The implementation of the goal will make a real difference to the participants, their team, and the company, and the goals must be directly related: The goal flows out of the course content.
Standard	An average or normal requirement, quality, quantity, level set for performance of a training program.
Success Gate	A value set as the prediction for training's results. Success Gates are created for Intention (goals and beliefs), Adoption, and Impact results.
Successful Adoption	Participants who self-report via a survey that they have completed their goal and what they have done is similar to an Adoptive Behavior from the Impact Matrix. Usually, a survey uses the following responses as a measure of *Successful Adoption*: (1) Completed: I do this all the time, or (2) Significant Progress: I am doing this most of the time.
Summary of Success Gate Data (Intention Dashboard)	Commentary from the evaluator that provides additional data on the Intention results.
Survey	A formal or official examination of the particulars of a training program, made in order to ascertain Adoption and Impact results.
Unrealized Value	This is a conclusion drawn from the Low-Impact group asking *"What if this group were as successful as the High-Impact group?"*

Notes

Chapter 1

1 American Society of Training and Development, "The Value of Evaluation: Making Training Evaluations More Effective." An ASTD Research Study, 2009.

2 Most participants in the corporate world have a choice if they attend a course or not—usually as part of their development plan. So you hope that they have some intent on using the training (unless they do not have a choice but must take the course).

Chapter 2

1 Tracy, Brian (2003, 2004). *Goals! How to Get Everything You Want—Faster Than You Ever Thought Possible.* San Francisco: Berrett-Koehler Publishers.

2 Butler, Ava S. (1996). *Team Think.* New York: McGraw-Hill.

3 Fletcher, A. (2002). *FireStarter Youth Power Curriculum: Participant Guidebook.* Olympia, WA: Freechild Project.

4 The time value of money is the value of money figuring in a given amount of interest earned over a given amount of time. For example, 100 dollars of today's money invested for one year and earning 5 percent interest will be worth 105 dollars after one year. Therefore, 100 dollars paid now or 105 dollars paid exactly one year from now both have the same value to the recipient, who assumes 5 percent interest; using time value of money terminology, 100 dollars invested for one year at 5 percent interest has a future value of 105 dollars.

Chapter 3

1 Used with permission from Dr. Marguerite Foxon, Performance Improvement Consulting.

Chapter 5

1 Predictive Evaluation provides a summary of how to analyze survey data. To learn more, please reference the following: Fink, Arlene (1995). *How to Analyze Survey Data.* Thousand Oaks, CA: SAGE Publications, Inc.

2 This book is not designed to teach statistics. An excellent source is this text: Jaeger, Richard M. (1983). *Statistics a Spectator Sport.* Beverly Hills, CA: Sage Publications.

3 These steps within Impact Evaluation are based on Rob Brinkerhoff's The Success Case Method. Brinkerhoff, R. O. (2003). *The Success Case Method: Find Out Quickly What's Working and What's Not*. San Francisco: Berrett-Koehler Publishers.

4 Wheeler, Patricia, Haertel, Geneva D., Scriven, Michael. (1992). *Teacher Evaluation Glossary*. Kalamazoo, MI: CREATE Project, The Evaluation Center, Western Michigan University.

Bibliography and Recommended Readings

Predictive Evaluation has been developed out of Dave Basarab's personal experiences and evaluation work, as well as drawing from the following sources:

Basarab, D. J., & Root, D. (1992). *The Training Evaluation Process.* Boston/Dordrecht/London: Kluwer Academic Publishers.

Brinkerhoff, R. O., & Apking, A. M. (2001). *High Impact Learning.* Cambridge: Persus Publishing.

Brinkerhoff, R. O. (2003). *The Success Case Method: Find Out Quickly What's Working and What's Not.* San Francisco: Berrett-Koehler Publishers.

Butler, Ava S. (1996). *Team Think.* New York: McGraw-Hill.

Dick, W., & Carey, L. (1996). *The Systematic Design of Instruction (4th Ed.).* New York: Harper Collins College Publishers.

Fink, Arlene (1995). *How to Analyze Survey Data.* Thousand Oaks, CA: SAGE Publications, Inc.

Fletcher, A. (2002). *FireStarter Youth Power Curriculum: Participant Guidebook.* Olympia, WA: Freechild Project.

Jaeger, Richard M. (1983). *Statistics a Spectator Sport:* Beverly Hills, CA: Sage Publications.

Kirkpatrick, D. L. (1998). *Evaluating Training Programs*, Second Edition. San Francisco: Berrett-Koehler Publishers.

Leshin, C. B., Pollock, J., & Reigeluth, C. M. (1992). *Instructional Design Strategies and Tactics.* Englewood Cliffs, NJ: Education Technology Publications.

Russ, Darlene F., Bober, Marcie J., Teja, Ilena, Foxon, Marguerite (2008). *Evaluator Competencies: Standards for the Practice of Evaluation.* San Francisco, CA: Jossey-Bass, Inc.

Swanson, Richard A., Gradous, Deane B. (1988). *Forecasting Financial Benefits of Human Resource Development.* San Francisco, CA: Jossey-Bass, Inc.

Wheeler, Patricia, Haertel, Geneva D., Scriven, Michael. (1992). *Teacher Evaluation Glossary.* Kalamazoo, MI: CREATE Project, The Evaluation Center, Western Michigan University.

Acknowledgments

Over the years, my passion for training and, specifically, for evaluation has grown, and I have dedicated my professional life to making these disciplines a little bit better. Many people have taught me the skills that I needed to be successful and provided me with the opportunities to practice them.

For assisting me in gaining the skills necessary to be able to learn my lessons, I'd like to thank Arnold Margerum, Warren Purude, Ron Larsen, Don Kirkpatrick, John Marohl, Bill Wiggenhorn, Brenda Sumberg, Ron Gemkow, Gary Langley, Pam Bossert, Kevin Weiss, Ed Hefferenan, Keith Wyche, Alfredo Doereste, Rob Brinkerhoff, Lois Webster, and Rita Smith.

The people who showed up and helped me create PE were angels. I thank Jim Kirkpatrick, Dr. Randy Bennett, and Dr. Roy Pollack for reviewing early drafts and providing guidance and feedback.

Finally, I deeply thank Dr. Marguerite Foxon, my friend and evaluation partner. Together we practiced and honed PE into its current form. She made sure that what we did made sense and spent countless hours reading manuscripts and offering awesome suggestions for improvement. She made this book so much better. She is a close personal friend, and I will forever be indebted to her.

Index

About the Author

Dave Basarab has been in training and development for thirty-six years, and he has been a practicing evaluator for twenty-five years.

Dave Basarab graduated from The University of Akron School of Education with a degree in Secondary Mathematics and Business Education. He received his Masters Degree in Educational Administration from the University of Dayton. For the first five years of his career, he taught math and business in Kettering, Ohio.

In 1979, Dave Basarab used his education experience to take on the development and instruction of customer and systems engineering training for NCR Corporation's emerging application software business: developing and teaching numerous courses—some classroom based, others in the emerging technology of e-learning. In 1988, Dave led the course development function for NCR and began its first evaluations, eventually developing its global evaluation methodology.

In 1991, Dave Basarab joined Motorola, managing the Evaluation Department for Motorola University. Here he further expanded his evaluation expertise and published his first book, with Dr. Darrel Root, *The Training Evaluation Process,* along with several evaluation articles. During his tenure at Motorola, he held numerous leadership roles in the Semiconductor Products Sectors business unit and the University.

In 2001, Dave Basarab led the Employee Development and Performance organization for Pitney Bowes mailing systems unit. Here he led a team of learning professionals, and the department received a prestigious ranking in Training's Top 100 for 2005. Dave was featured in a 2005 *Wall Street Journal* article on using business simulations in leadership development and was awarded the "2005 Learning Innovation Award" from *Chief Learning Officer* magazine.

In 2005, Dave Basarab led Ingersoll Rand's Global Leadership College for Ingersoll Rand University.

In 2007, Dave Basarab founded V.A.L.E. Consulting, LLC, which offers PE services to global customers, partnering with them and providing evaluation studies of the highest quality in a cost-effective manner. Evaluations are fully customizable and unique to their courses. Dave also provides PE workshops (classroom or Webinars) that teach training evaluation expertise so that you will be able to conduct a PE and evaluate Intention, Adoption, and Impact. All courses are fully customized to meet your needs. Dave also provides evaluation coaching on predicting training value, performing Intention, Adoption, and Impact evaluations.

If you wish to have a PE conducted on your training, attend a workshop, or receive evaluation coaching, contact Dave at valelearn@gmail.com or visit www.evaluatetraining.com.

Also, in 2007, Dave cofounded P&D Learning, LLC, which offers business acumen training—delivered by Learning Bursts that teach essential financial concepts, marketing, and innovation and are explained in eight- to ten-minute audio segments , accompanied by a workbook of simple explanations and practical exercises and reinforced with a business simulation that enables learners to apply what they have learned. For inquiries on business acumen training, visit www.learningbursts.com.

Berrett–Koehler
Publishers

Berrett-Koehler is an independent publisher dedicated to an ambitious mission: *Creating a World That Works for All*.

We believe that to truly create a better world, action is needed at all levels—individual, organizational, and societal. At the individual level, our publications help people align their lives with their values and with their aspirations for a better world. At the organizational level, our publications promote progressive leadership and management practices, socially responsible approaches to business, and humane and effective organizations. At the societal level, our publications advance social and economic justice, shared prosperity, sustainability, and new solutions to national and global issues.

A major theme of our publications is "Opening Up New Space." Berrett-Koehler titles challenge conventional thinking, introduce new ideas, and foster positive change. Their common quest is changing the underlying beliefs, mindsets, institutions, and structures that keep generating the same cycles of problems, no matter who our leaders are or what improvement programs we adopt.

We strive to practice what we preach—to operate our publishing company in line with the ideas in our books. At the core of our approach is stewardship, which we define as a deep sense of responsibility to administer the company for the benefit of all of our "stakeholder" groups: authors, customers, employees, investors, service providers, and the communities and environment around us.

We are grateful to the thousands of readers, authors, and other friends of the company who consider themselves to be part of the "BK Community." We hope that you, too, will join us in our mission.

A BK Business Book

This book is part of our BK Business series. BK Business titles pioneer new and progressive leadership and management practices in all types of public, private, and nonprofit organizations. They promote socially responsible approaches to business, innovative organizational change methods, and more humane and effective organizations.

Berrett–Koehler
Publishers

A community dedicated to creating
a world that works for all

Visit Our Website: www.bkconnection.com

Read book excerpts, see author videos and Internet movies, read our authors' blogs, join discussion groups, download book apps, find out about the BK Affiliate Network, browse subject-area libraries of books, get special discounts, and more!

Subscribe to Our Free E-Newsletter, the *BK Communiqué*

Be the first to hear about new publications, special discount offers, exclusive articles, news about bestsellers, and more! Get on the list for our free e-newsletter by going to **www.bkconnection.com**.

Get Quantity Discounts

Berrett-Koehler books are available at quantity discounts for orders of ten or more copies. Please call us toll-free at (800) 929-2929 or email us at bkp.orders@ aidcvt.com.

Join the BK Community

BKcommunity.com is a virtual meeting place where people from around the world can engage with kindred spirits to create a world that works for all. **BKcommunity** .com members may create their own profiles, blog, start and participate in forums and discussion groups, post photos and videos, answer surveys, announce and register for upcoming events, and chat with others online in real time. Please join the conversation!

Mixed Sources
Product group from well-managed
forests, controlled sources and
recycled wood or fiber
www.fsc.org Cert no. SW-COC-003925
© 1996 Forest Stewardship Council
FSC